D0340050

Tell Him That I Heard

Patricia Hangen

Tell
Him
That
I Heard

HARPER & ROW, PUBLISHERS

New York, Hagerstown, San Francisco, London

FIRST EDITION

Designed by Stephanie Krasnow

Library of Congress Cataloging in Publication Data

Hangen, Patricia.
    Tell him that I heard.
    1. Hangen, Welles, 1930-   2. Journalists—
United States—Biography. 3. Hangen, Patricia.
4. Wives—United States—Biography. I. Title.
PN4874.H224H3   070'.92'4 [B]   76-40581
ISBN 0-06-011788-5

77 78 79 80 10 9 8 7 6 5 4 3 2 1

For Welles

1

The Commitment

The majestic old white house is hard to spot when you scan the ascent of Victoria Peak from a boat in Hong Kong harbor. Half-way up, standing proudly among thick trees, its high arched windows and tall chimneys seem all but obscured by verdant climbers.

But let your eye follow the course taken by Hong Kong's peak tram. The track shoots straight up the mountain for two-thirds of its climb and then jaunts off obliquely to the right. Find that divergent point, then look slightly to the left along the wooded slope. Fix on a shape of white gables which appears to be seeking seclusion.

There. You have it. This is the venerable colonial house that is our Hong Kong home.

This graceful place is a remnant of the days when Britannia ruled the waves, and in order to live there one must be incurably romantic, or exceedingly warm-blooded. The rooms are cavernous, with twenty-foot ceilings and deep fireplaces all around. Half the rambling structure is unusable because it comprises the catacombed servants' quarters of decades past. But its handsome glassed-in porticos overlooking all of Hong Kong harbor make it a historian's haven. And what is a good newsman after all but an unusually perceptive historian, a beat ahead of his time?

My husband, Welles, is just such a newsman, which is why we fell in love with our looming anachronism on sight. We were assigned to Hong Kong in early 1966 so that Welles could head the NBC News bureau there, and we were able to move into the house shortly after our arrival. The porous stucco façade had walled up such a clammy chill that no one else wanted it. The first thing we did was to light all the fireplaces in the house and we lived in overcoats that whole first month, but finally the old place accepted the fact that it no longer sheltered Englishmen and began to warm up.

For us, its character continued to outweigh its discomforts. It was strictly old British Raj: aloof from the Colony's masses, yet with an overview that allowed no disturbance to pass unnoticed. There was even the weathered status-symbol flagpole which, in other times, flew the company pennant of the wealthy "taipan" then in residence.

That sort of character melted long ago in nostalgia, but I believe that we left our own mark on its personality as well, in the days before Welles went away. They were times of boundless fulfillment, for we love each other and share a devotion to our profession. We lived every day to the fullest, and savored the happiness of the long evenings in front of our blazing hearth. Often with friends, but more often alone.

The news business is a kind of obsession. Once embraced, it fills your life. It means living events as they happen and investing every sense in trying to find the truth and understand. Only then can events be interpreted to others. It is often hazardous, but committing oneself completely to any pursuit involves hazard.

A dedicated newsman loves truth as much as life and, despite the risks he runs, would agree with Shakespeare's Julius Caesar that it seems most strange that man should fear. The words of this moving soliloquy have always lived in my husband's heart:

> Cowards die many times before their deaths;
> The valiant never taste of death but once.
> Of all the wonders that I yet have heard,
> It seems to me most strange that men should fear;
> Seeing that death, a necessary end,
> Will come when it will come.

So when Welles disappeared into the jungles of Cambodia that day, in search of truth, I understood his commitment and my heart went with him. I do not understand the enigma that holds him there still. But one day my heart will return from those silent jungles, well-nurtured by enduring love.

Our old white house waits in quiet patience, as if it too knows that this hiatus in life will pass. For our chapter in its history has not yet been fully written.

Welles was just eighteen when his devotion to the news began. He had graduated from Brown University with honors in 1948, but his Kansas-bred parents wisely recognized his need for further education in living in the world and in life itself and they urged him to travel. His French was fluent so it seemed logical for him to head for Paris.

The world's leaders were gathered in Geneva right then trying to pound out a format for keeping peace, and the Paris *Herald* needed extra hands to cover the story. Welles applied and was sent there on his first reporting assignment. No salary, of course, but with his lack of experience, he viewed it as a great break and went off in high excitement. The *Herald* liked his work and soon hired him as a full-time correspondent.

The Paris *Herald* was to newsmen of the Forties what Gertrude Stein's salon was to other writers in an earlier time. Many of the journalists best known today were brought up there, for the editors were intent on encouraging bright new talent and the City Room was a place of congenial inspiration. There Welles learned the skills and joys of reporting.

It was not long before the *New York Times* offered him a place in its Frankfurt bureau, with the opportunity to become chief if he proved capable. Welles went, loved the work, and devoted himself to it and to becoming proficient in German. The post was soon his.

After that he was assigned the *Times* bureau in Ankara, Turkey, and our paths were set on their fated course of encounter.

We had not met in those days when Welles was in Paris learning his profession. I was studying at Stanford University and had not yet found a major interest, much less any dedication. My parents, who had grown up in Nebraska before deciding to toss their caps over the windmill called "California," had worked so hard to get me to Stanford that I felt I owed them a return. College was great fun, but when I graduated it seemed only right that I repay their love and trust by getting a job and supporting myself for a change.

New York seemed the most intriguing place to begin. Three friends and I found an apartment there at the northern tip of Manhattan, so far from the center of town that even the subways panted. It was a great place, right out of *My Sister Eileen.* We didn't even have to go outdoors to tell the weather; we knew by the feet passing our lone window situated up near the ceiling. We couldn't see the people, just their feet; if those feet wore galoshes, we had rain. Dining was strictly tuna-noodle casserole all the way. But we felt that we were really living.

My first job was with the *Ladies' Home Journal* where the eccentric but brilliant Wilhela Cushman, then fashion editor, began my real education. She taught me the basics of writing and how to look and listen, so when my longing for San Francisco compelled my return, I was able to go to work on the *Examiner.* My commitment to the news business grew when I went to Athens four years later as a press officer in the American Embassy. And it was there, during a series of earthquakes that almost demolished southern Greece, that I found Welles.

Or rather, he found me.

I can still see him as he walked into my office that day. His tanned face was damp from the Athens humidity, but his light brown hair was smoothed back as though he had whisked a comb through it just before entering. It was an intelligent face, broad-boned, finely lined. And when he smiled, his whole face took part and his eyes shone.

"Hello," he said, striding across the room to my desk. "Welles Hangen, *New York Times.* I hope you're the press officer." He seemed to tower over the desk as he stood smiling down at me.

"No, sorry, he's out for the moment," I said, smiling back. "I'm his assistant, Pat Dana. What may I do to help?"

"I've just come in from Ankara," he said, sitting down in the chair opposite me. "I'm hoping for some late details on the earthquake."

Patras, a port city in the southern Peloponnesos, had suffered the latest shocks, and I was able to give him the facts and figures on those. I felt terribly competent, really quite pleased with myself.

"Thanks," Welles said then, "you've been very helpful. I guess I'll go on down there and see what's happened."

"But I just told you," I said, surprised. "There's no reason to make the trip. You have it all right there."

"I can't report how it looks if I don't see it," he said, closing his notebook. "I'll be back by the end of the week. See you then." And he strode back out the door.

Very attractive, I thought, watching him go. *Very* attractive . . . but a bit odd. Who would want to go to a ruined city like Patras if he didn't have to? But the more I thought about it, the more sense it made. A reporter is no reporter at all if he relies only on government handouts or someone else's word.

I thought about him a lot while he was gone, and the more I thought about him, the more I liked him. How could I keep the story going so he would stay longer in Greece?

When the earth stopped shaking and Welles returned to Athens, he appeared again in my office. "I'd like to check around a bit more before I leave," he said with that same engaging smile. "And I'll need your help, if you will. Could we talk it over at dinner? I'd like to take in a taverna if you'll go with me."

We closed three or four tavernas that night, as I recall. Maybe even more. Because Welles' thoughts about the responsibilities of reporting and his determination to find the truth, *and* his excitement when he found it and got the story out, were so contagious that I could have talked forever. So when we said good night, I suggested that he might want to visit a Greek island the next day. There could be another earthquake story there. Would he want to miss that?

"Will you go with me?" he asked.

We sailed to Euboea the next morning. Our ideas continued to spill out, to splash, to overlap, as we wandered that quiet island. We were now thoughtful, now bursting with laughter, now thoughtful again. So much to talk about, so little time.

"You know?" Welles said that night as we sat under the stars at a seaside taverna, "you'd make a damned good reporter yourself. Why don't you stop being a government spokesman? Come over to *my* side of the desk. It's a terrific way to live. And we could *really* soar, together."

It was as if I had been fumbling for a match all my life, and had finally hit the main switch that lit up the heavens.

For Welles had a commitment to *live*. It was as simple and as beautiful as that. I had just begun to share it. Every day an adventure, every sight significant, every experience whole. Life could be humorous, moving, even tragic. But the morbid was always refused, the mundane dismissed out of hand. And I would be privileged to share it all. Privileged, above all, to know him well. Hence my story.

2

Reporting the Hard Way

Welles and I were married in Cairo where he had come to cover Middle Eastern news for NBC. Our civil ceremony, required by Egyptian law, had all the romantic allure of a small claims court and had I not been halfway around the world, I might well have gone home. Most brides are nervous, but when you are nervous in Arabic you are in deep trouble. But I had woven enough romantic dreams into this day to carry me along, and when we were finally alone with only the dazzling path of moonlight on the Nile River for company, suddenly and surely all was right with us and with our world.

In those early days I felt that being married to a foreign correspondent was a little like living on the lip of an active volcano. Since then, it has seemed more like a precipice: there is no way of knowing when you might be moving on. So, in your head at least, your bags are always packed. You keep your bills paid up to the day. And you try never ever to make any long-range plans.

We had been married just two weeks when Welles came home with a cable. I was still unpacking dishes and books, hanging up pictures and then moving them, and was even euphoric enough to be enjoying ladies' coffee parties. I could not have been happier. But then he spoke.

"Looks like something is happening in Lebanon," Welles said, casually tossing the cable on a stack of pictures. "Let's go up there and see."

"Fine, dear," I said, after a kiss. "Sounds like fun. When do you want to go?" I figured that we could be free in about ten days.

"The plane leaves at seven-thirty in the morning," he said, "so we should probably start packing because we will have to get out there early. Are my shirts back from the laundry?"

Back from the laundry? I hadn't even sent them yet. Until this moment the two in his drawer had seemed enough to me.

But we were on that plane to Beirut the next morning, by which time I had learned my lesson the hard way—over an ironing board heaped with soggy shirts.

That was 1958. Egypt's Suez Canal battles had already taken place. The sky was falling all over the Middle East. Tiny affluent Lebanon seemed to be the next in the chain of Arab countries to be tested, so we were heading for Beirut to investigate.

I shall never forget that drive from Beirut airport into town. The broad boulevards and twisting side streets were deserted except for a few stalking policemen. Windows were tightly shuttered, even against the sea. And soldiers sat rigidly in parked trucks, their guns across their knees.

Never having been in Beirut before, I didn't miss the motor and pedestrian traffic that normally jams those streets. But it was clear that something was wrong. There was no one about except militia. And then a rock stung our windshield!

Our car was moving swiftly along the Mediterranean coast road leading toward town when a crude barricade of rocks and tree branches loomed ahead. It appeared to have been hastily thrown together and was not enough to stop us. But we were slowed down enough to be pelted by a band of ragged children hurling stones from the embankment above. We learned later that they were being paid for their work by older hoodlums we were soon to meet in town.

We edged our car around the debris and sped on into Beirut. Here we found professional barbed-wire barricades blocking side streets. Echoes of sporadic shooting came from the center of town, and anxious people were hurrying to cover. We had to resort to narrow back alleys in order to reach our hotel safely.

Finally there it was: the imposing St. Georges Hotel, stolidly defying trouble of any sort by stretching its fences protectively around the sunbathers on its private beach and the gliding sailboats in its harbor. Speedboat motors drowned out sounds of the shooting downtown.

Joseph, the imperious concierge, shifted his bulky frame and watched us dourly as we entered his lobby. A room? We could have a whole floor if we wished. He shot a withering glance at the departing tourists whose luggage crowded the entrance, implying that he had little use for travelers who flee with their dollars at the merest whiff of trouble. His baleful glare showed his displeasure at getting journalists as replacements.

But we were too excited to care. Welles hurried off to find out what was happening in town, and I went up to our room to unpack.

Welles had been a foreign correspondent for nearly ten years, and had learned to pack a dozen shirts and five suits even if he was only going across the street. There was no way of knowing when a news assignment might end. I was still a bride, and deciding which of my treasured trousseau to take had been too much for me, so I packed everything. Now, ringing for more hangers, I began the pleasant task of sorting our clothes and getting our room in order. But half an hour later I had finished. There was nothing to do then but wait.

Four hours later Welles returned, tie askew, hair tousled, and filled with enthusiasm.

"It might be something really big," he said breathlessly. "Barricades all over town. Shooting around the Presidency. Snipers everywhere. It looks like the Opposition is out to get Chamoun. Saeb Salam is hiding out in the old section. He has the whole area barricaded off by his henchmen." He was pacing the room with excitement.

But these names meant nothing to me. I was furious at having been left alone for so long. Married only two weeks and I was already taking second place to a bunch of snipers. Beirut for me was losing its glamor fast.

"Looks like a terrific story," Welles exclaimed. Then, missing my mood completely, he added, "Aren't you glad we came!"

9

I couldn't look at him. I stared angrily at the Mediterranean instead. It is possible to cope with almost anything if you can look at a serene blue sea, and very soon the whole thing seemed ridiculous. Here I was, resolutely ignoring my husband, and he was too excited to know that he was being ignored. Maybe waiting alone in a hotel room for hours was not *my* idea of wedded bliss, but he obviously was not aware of it. So, I said to myself and to the sea, maybe I had better do something about it.

"Welles," I interrupted, turning toward him, "please stop a minute. I want to know what is happening, but not *this* way. I want to be with you when you are finding out, instead of just waiting for you. Couldn't we do it together?"

"Why sure, honey," he said, surprised. "I thought that you wanted to unpack and get some rest. You can come along anytime, you know that. I'd like that better too. Unless it is dangerous. I wouldn't want you in anything dangerous."

"Well *I* would," I said quickly. "I'd take danger anytime as long as we're together."

"All right," Welles said with a quick smile, "you're on! But now will you please listen? If you are going to help, you'll need a few facts. For instance: Camille Chamoun is president of Lebanon."

"Okay, smarty, I have that one. What else do you know?"

Welles briefed me quickly then. Chamoun was completing his sixth year in office and meant to run for a second term. This was unpopular with the Opposition. His enemies meant to force him to resign and didn't care what tactics they might have to use. Saeb Salam, leader of the Opposition, was calling the shots.

"It could be just a skirmish," he continued, "except for one thing: Chamoun is Christian, and Salam and friends are Moslem. It could turn into communal war."

This I understood and it was indeed serious. Lebanon is the last stronghold for Christians in the area where Christ was born. It had always maintained a population balance between Christians and Moslems, the former holding most business interests and the latter farming. Now this precarious balance was endan-

10

gered not only by a disproportionate birthrate among the Moslems and the emigration of Christians, but also by open Moslem hostility.

"It could be an important story," Welles went on. "Clearly the government expects trouble. They have imposed a curfew to keep people off the streets, but I have passes for us so we can get through the police."

"You mean you had a curfew pass for me all the time?" I asked, feeling foolish about my earlier hurt. "Darling, thank you. You *are* wonderful. When do we begin?"

When we began was that very afternoon.

Welles scheduled a broadcast for five P.M. to be transmitted directly to New York from the telephone-telegraph office in downtown Beirut. Given the time differential, NBC listeners in the States would have the news in mid-morning.

And news there was. Seven people killed in street fighting in Beirut . . . rumors that Syrians were infiltrating to aid the Opposition . . . accusations that Nasser's push for Arab nationalism was behind it all . . . appeals to be made to the United Nations . . . clandestine rebel radio stations operating from the mountains . . . guerrilla bands accosting travelers on the Beirut-Damascus highway.

Welles talked to dozens of people on both sides of the political fence and we took another tour of town just before curfew to get the latest picture. Then came the script writing, which seemed the hardest part to me. Welles had to write the story in concise segments, each timed at exactly forty-five seconds, to be broadcast on NBC hourly news programs throughout the day. Instead of a single lead sentence for the whole story, he needed one for each separate report. It was writing a news story the hard way, but he was good at it and quick, so soon we were ready to go.

It was four P.M. The broadcast was scheduled an hour from then, but we wanted to have plenty of time in case we had trouble getting through this nervous city. The broadcasting facilities were in the heart of town, nearly half an hour away from our hotel by taxi. That is, if we could get a taxi.

11

"Very sorry, sir." Joseph beamed at his concierge desk. "Taxi drivers are too frightened to drive this late. It is almost curfew. There is no way for you to get to the cable office now." He looked happier than he had looked all day.

Welles remonstrated, shouted, banged the desk. Joseph just shrugged happily, repeating, "Sorry, no way." Nothing pleased him more than to be justifiably unable to help.

"Come on," Welles said to me. "We'll walk!" And off we went, stomping out of the bright St. Georges lobby into the dim, quiet street.

We did walk for a while. Or rather, I jogged. Welles has one of the longest strides I have ever tried to keep up with. Then fortunately an off-duty taxi came up the street. The driver was eager to get home before curfew, but even more eager to arrive there with some extra dollars in his pocket, so he agreed reluctantly to take us to the cable office. We climbed in, and the driver started up Beirut's narrow streets, past shuttered residences pockmarked by sniper fire, into the center of town. He made no secret of his fear of the downtown area, and careened through the streets like a runaway horse. Depositing us at the cable office entrance, he clearly reproached us for placing his life in jeopardy. Welles tried to reassure him by pointing out that there was no shooting anywhere nearby, that obviously this area was the safest in town, and that we expected him to wait for us. Grumbling, he switched off the motor and slumped down low in his seat. His distrustful eyes peered bleakly over the window ledge as we hurried off.

Beirut's broadcasting facilities occupied one wing of the cable office, two flights up. I headed for the elevator but Welles was already mounting the stairs at a gallop.

"It's quicker this way," he called. "If the elevator is as old as this building, we'll miss the circuit entirely." And he raced on ahead, leaving me a very poor second. By the time I had cleared the last step, Welles was already inside talking to the director.

"I'll try to get New York right now," the alert Lebanese said as he disappeared into the control room. We could hear him calling, "Hello, New York. Hello, New York. Come in, please."

Then a voice came through on the New York circuit.

"Hangen? Is that you? You're right on time," said the voice from New York. "Go ahead please with your voice level."

"Five . . . four . . . three . . . two . . . one . . . testing," began Welles, facing a microphone on the small table. He adjusted his headphones and straightened his pile of scripts, preparing to broadcast.

"Voice level okay," said the voice. "Go ahead."

"The opening skirmishes of what could become a full-scale revolution broke out today in Beirut, Lebanon," Welles read. "President Camille Chamoun is a virtual prisoner since fighting began early today around his home. The Opposition demands his resignation in the face of widespread violence which has already erupted throughout this frightened city. . . ."

Thirty minutes later, Welles' work was done. Technicians in the New York studios tape-recorded his broadcasts for use in America throughout the day: the first reports of Lebanon's emerging revolution.

"Thanks, Mr. Habib," Welles said, shaking the director's hand. "See you tomorrow."

At that moment we heard the first shot.

The sound cut the silence of the street below our window, and in a flash the air exploded with machinegun fire. Mr. Habib pushed us back from the window and curtained it. Then he grabbed his pistol from a desk drawer and disappeared. Shouts in the office corridors, shots from the street, and there we stood staring at each other. Welles raced to the window and looked through the curtains. Snipers lined the rooftops opposite. Men were running crazily through the street, firing at others coming from doorways and around corners. A grenade demolished a curbed automobile. The street was a scene of chaos.

Suddenly in bounced Mr. Habib, looking gleeful.

"Got two," he crowed. "From the roof."

"You?" I asked, incredulous at the thought of this serious gentleman ducking behind roof chimneys. He nodded happily.

"How much longer do you think this will last?" asked Welles, with an amount of concern that surprised me. He seemed as

13

worried as I, and I was touched to think that it was probably my safety that alarmed him.

"No more than a few hours, I guess," Mr. Habib said calmly. "You will be safe here. Both sides in this war use our facilities, so they won't hurt *this* building. May I offer you each a coffee?"

Welles frowned, looked at his watch, and thought a moment. Then: "No, but thanks," he said, starting toward the door. "There is still time for another circuit. Set it up for two hours from now, will you please? I'll go out and see what's happening." He had the door open now and beckoned to me.

"Come on, Pat," he said. "Let's go."

Mr. Habib begged him to reconsider, but Welles was firm. I simply thought: Well, anything for a story! and followed him to the door.

Then the worried director said, "Please allow Madame to stay here with me, in any case. I shall take care of her until you return."

Welles thought that was a fine idea, but I didn't. I'm covering this thing too, I thought. With you. So I shook my head quickly and hurried after him. We thanked Mr. Habib and left. But not quite fast enough to avoid his mournful eyes, which had the intent dreamy look of someone listening to music. A requiem, for instance.

The street was suddenly deserted when we stepped into its ominous quiet. Our taxi driver had fled, so we had our footwork cut out. Staying close to the wall, we walked as fast as we could through those streets. Downhill seemed the best course. That way we would have to come to the waterfront eventually and then could work our way along it to the hotel.

My high heels clack-clacked along the silent streets. The narrow winding avenues were quiet and shuttered, and my footsteps echoed loudly.

"Shhh!" Welles frowned, and I tried to tiptoe. But full stride requires leading with the heel so it was a question of clattering or standing still.

"They wouldn't hurt a foreigner anyway," I murmured, skipping a few steps to keep up.

14

"Anyone can tell we are Christian a mile away," he answered. My bangs glued themselves to my forehead at that gem of consolation.

Right then we came to the dead-end of our street, but directly ahead was an open garden gate with steps leading down to the continuing street below. The garden was bright with flamingo trees, which I usually love. But these seemed the perfect perch for snipers, so I hurried past Welles, running down the last few steps and heading for the street. He took the steps in one leap and caught me in the gateway. I had never seen him so angry. I returned his glare, thinking that he had a lot of nerve to be mad at *me*. Who got us into this anyway, I thought, and I was just about to say so when he stepped past me into the street and scanned both sides to make sure that we had not stumbled into firing range. Then, satisfied that all was clear, he returned.

"Look, baby," he began sternly, "I have to get you back to the hotel. And fast. But we are not going to make it if we take stupid chances. Now will you please just calm down and *follow* me."

On we went, aiming crow-fashion for our hotel. Still complete silence. Still no people. This was a narrow street that curved at the far end. It was lined with high apartment buildings that blocked our line of sight. We kept close to the walls on the shady side and were approaching the blind curve when Welles stopped me with a sudden outstretched arm. I followed his gaze up to the top floor of a building opposite. There, leaning from a curtained window, was a man waving frantically with both arms, urging us back. It was a grotesque pantomime in that silent street, but the meaning was clear: there was danger around the curve. We were to get out of there fast.

Signaling to show that we had understood and appreciated his warning, we retraced our steps and ducked into the first open doorway we could find. Just in time. Welles pulled me to shelter as a barrage of machinegun fire split the air. The far end of the street erupted in shooting. Had it not been for the stranger in the window, we would have been right in the middle of it. We hid there until the gunmen chased each other on to some

15

other street and then we raced for the uphill corner, turned it, and were on our way again as more firing began behind us.

Finally, there ahead of us was the St. Georges and we both broke into a run. Safety at last!

Once back in our room, Welles began working the phones to get the latest uptown developments before his broadcast. I ordered a cup of tea and took it out on our balcony overlooking the sea, hoping to get my nerves settled after that frightening scramble home. How peaceful it was: dusk, water skiers and sailboats still performing on the waves below, a gentle cooling breeze. I took a deep breath, a sip of tea, and reflected on all that I had learned this day. While I had been running through those streets, hoping to get away from danger by heading straight for the hotel, Welles had selected the longer course, putting the city's central district behind us by aiming for the quiet waterfront. He silently scanned every street before permitting us to enter, and kept constant vigil as we progressed. He knew what we had to do, but was allowing no risks along the way. I marveled at his calmness, and felt a great surge of pride and confidence in this man whom I had been lucky enough to marry.

Then his voice broke my reverie. Roused, I got up and stepped inside, merely to find him fuming over some wrong phone numbers.

But at that moment we both froze. A bullet *zzzinged* across our balcony.

Perhaps it was simply too anticlimactic for me—and even Welles said that it sounded like a spent bullet, an obvious mistake—so I was ready to shrug it off. But right then my darling husband went into a tantrum. The firing around the cable office had not fazed him; that chaotic street fighting had left his nerves untouched. But this! He became almost apoplectic and swiftly he laid down the law: I was never to go out on that balcony again! What in the world had I thought I was doing, sitting out there with no protection? I could have been shot!

That was the only time I can remember when Welles' sense of humor deserted him. And I don't think he ever understood why I found it so terribly funny.

16

3

The Great Big Saw

At this point Abdullah came into our lives.

Abdullah is a taxi driver in Beirut. At least he was during the revolution, but since half the town accused him of being in the pay of the government and the other half was convinced that he was a rebel, nobody knows what happened to him when peace came again.

He looked like a swarthy Assyrian Jack Dempsey, weighing in at two hundred twenty or so and all muscle. He drove a new fire-engine-red Chrysler and drove it expertly with a lifetime knowledge of Lebanon's winding roads and back alleys.

For both reasons, Abdullah was the foreign correspondent's dream when anyone contemplated a trip outside Beirut into the guerrilla-filled mountains. He knew his way around and he knew whom to bribe. And if either talent failed, he had two leaded fists with lots behind them.

Lebanon's revolution was only a few weeks old when newspaper readers were shocked awake one morning by reports of a massacre at the Syrian border. An unidentified raiding party had swooped across that border from Syria in the night, murdered five guards in the Lebanese customs shed, and then bombed and burned it. Seven gasoline tank trucks, caught in customs, exploded and their drivers were killed. The Lebanese customs area was an inferno for hours and there were no survivors.

The crime stirred up bitter resentment among the Lebanese against Syria and solidified opinion that the rebels were getting aid from the East. It also closed the border for several weeks, and created a no-man's-land some fifteen miles broad between the two countries. But no one yet knew who was responsible.

For some strange reason, Welles chose this inauspicious moment to want to visit Damascus. And he saw no reason for flying since it was only a three-hour drive over the mountains from Beirut.

"Was," I corrected, waving my newspaper across the breakfast table.

"What was what?" he asked rather indistinctly between bites of toast.

"Well, I gather from this story that somebody blew up the road last night," I said. "It's going to take a lot longer than three hours to make it now."

"I wonder if that is true," he said thoughtfully. "Let's go up there and see what really did happen. Find out who did it and why. Might be interesting to see if we can make it through."

"But we *can't* get through," I argued. "That's the whole point. Look, I like a good story too, but it says right here: murderers, bandits, outlaws. . . ."

"Don't you want to go with me?" he asked.

The next morning at six o'clock we were sitting in the back of Abdullah's long red taxi heading for Damascus.

I was trying hard to swallow my misgivings and to concentrate on the spectacular scenery, but Abdullah did not make it easy. First he took *all* of our money and my brand-new wedding ring and hid them in a special cache under the floorboards. Then he cautioned us to let him do all the talking no matter what happened . . . inevitably in a language neither of us understood. And then, the final straw: he would not be able to drive us beyond the Syrian border because Lebanese license plates would be suspect. But we were not to worry. He had arranged for a Syrian taxi to meet us there and take us on to Damascus. Me? I was sure that we were being sold into slavery.

The climb up over the Leban mountains *is* spectacular, however. The road lashes across fir and cedar cliffs, and with each switchback the view alternates between a widening panorama of Beirut on one side and mountain crevices and peaks on the other. Once over the summit, the road begins a long descent into Lebanon's fertile Bekáa Valley, which looks like a miniature of Austria's Inn Valley minus the river.

We began to have trouble right in the middle of that peaceful green valley. Nothing serious, just annoying. Every half mile the Lebanese Army had established checkpoints and each one demanded its due of time, polite smiles, identity cards, and unintelligible chit-chat. We became quite bored with these long before the fifteenth. But when we had cleared the sixteenth and heard Abdullah proclaim it the last army post on the Lebanese side of the border, tedium ended abruptly.

For this was no-man's-land. It stretched fifteen miles east from the far edge of the Bekáa Valley, through barren brown foothills dotted with sage and scrub, to the Syrian customs. There was no law left in those hills since the Lebanese Army withdrew to tighten its lines at the valley's edge after the customs massacre. And residents of the handful of hill villages had fled in the wake of the departing army.

As we drove slowly into bleak hills, we passed one such forlorn village whose cluster of mud-thatched houses had been deserted by their panicked owners. Deathly still, haunting, with a single stray dog whining plaintively.

The intrepid Abdullah drove on, never varying his thirty-five-miles-an-hour advance. It reminded me of that great big saw coming nearer and nearer as we went deeper into the hills. Nothing stirred, not even a breeze. I searched the hilltops around us, feeling exactly like the perilous Pauline herself.

"Listen carefully," Abdullah murmured over his shoulder. "If you hear anything, a voice or a shot, tell me."

That did it. I was scared now and moved closer to Welles. He put his arm around me, but continued to give his complete attention to the threatening silence around us. His vigilance was undivided. If the smallest leaf moved he would know it and, I felt sure, have me flat on the floor forthwith. I held my breath and listened.

We passed the gutted customs shed with its burned-out metal

remains, and crawled slowly on. No one said a word. The tension was almost unbearable but there was nothing to do but proceed.

Those were the longest fifteen miles I ever care to drive. Silent, oppressive, rife with sudden calamity. But we made it. As we rounded a bend on a hilltop, a bright metal sign loomed ahead: DOUANE—CUSTOMS. We had reached the Syrian border and no-man's-land was left behind.

Welles clapped Abdullah on the back and we all grinned with relief. Then I noticed that Abdullah's shirt was soaked with sweat. So our heavyweight champ had been scared too! The thought gave me chills even after the fact.

Syrian customs is among the most inhospitable in the world. There is always at least an hour's wait while black-list volumes are checked, and smiles are extremely rare. So we were prepared to encounter more trouble. But this day the inspectors rushed to meet us, smiling broadly. We were the first to make it through no-man's-land, along a road they thought was closed. We must be very important people indeed. They fell all over each other to please us.

Welles pressed the advantage and questioned them about the border massacre. They told him all about it, admitting that the raiding party was Syrian. They even gave him lists of arms shipments consigned to Lebanese rebels, all dated over the past week, all sent by the Syrian Army. I don't know how he kept from laughing out loud, but he did.

Then: "Now kindly stamp our visas right away," Welles said firmly. "We are late for an appointment with your president."

The effect was complete. Our passports were thrust back, the inspectors saluted, and we were implored to continue on in peace.

True to his word, Abdullah returned our money and my precious ring from the cache in his car, and turned us over to a Syrian taxi to continue our trip. We climbed in, looked around to make sure we had *really* made it, and then grinned at each other.

"Hi there, reporter," Welles said. "You're not bad at all."

20

"Takes one to know one," I said, smiling back at him. "At least
. . . life's never dull."

Welles planned to work on his scripts all the way down the
Syrian side of the mountain and on into Damascus, to be ready
for broadcasting as soon as we arrived. I knew that he wanted
to be left alone in order to concentrate on setting the story
straight. But there was one little matter which troubled me, and
I thought I'd better settle it while I still had a good bargaining
position, even if it meant bothering Welles for the next hour.

I began softly. "I'm sure glad that's over, aren't you? I never
want to take another drive like that one. Those empty hills. All
that ominous silence. Whew, I thought we would be attacked
any minute, didn't you? Weren't you frightened at all?"

"Hell, yes!" he laughed, glancing up from his work. "And I
don't want to drive back either. We'll fly in the morning, all
right? Now, will you *please* be quiet?"

"I wouldn't think of disturbing you, darling," I said with relief. And we drove on to Damascus in golden silence.

4

Wrong Time, Wrong Place

June was a bad month for Lebanon. Pitched battles between rebel bands and government army units terrorized the countryside. Battle areas spread from Tripoli in the north to the ancient southern port of Sidon. And Baalbek's towering Roman ruins in the east were being bombed into smaller, modern ruins. Beirut's harbor, long the prime entrepôt for the whole eastern Mediterranean, was closed completely. Even the famed American University of Beirut canceled its graduation exercises because large assemblies had become choice targets in the wave of bombings within the city.

Beirut's largest department store had been bombed and gutted because it had remained open for business in defiance of terrorist law. A packed streetcar was dynamited during rush hour, showering human debris over a block-long radius. Patrons of a downtown cafe met the same fate.

The city was terrorized. Shopkeepers did their meager business from backdoors in deep night to avoid frenzied retaliation. The American Embassy warned its personnel off the streets and made evacuation facilities available. Pan American's central office was bombed and most foreign businesses closed down immediately thereafter.

Oddly enough, our hotel area was not affected at all. Each time Welles and I returned there after taxi trips through town, it was like entering a different world. The St. Georges' beach was still dotted with sunbathers and the harbor was alive with pleasure craft. We often went down to swim in the late after-

22

noons. It was good relaxation after those tense spot-checks in town. Welles is a strong swimmer and often swam out farther into the sea than I liked, but he seemed to unwind that way and was better prepared for his broadcasts afterward. We left the water skiing to others. Not that we didn't enjoy it, but skimming over the waves in full view of snipers does leave something to be desired. And anyway, water skiing in the midst of a revolution seemed a bit of a paradox.

Rebel leaders, holed up in the barricaded Moslem quarter, blamed the government for the trouble in town. President Chamoun, a virtual prisoner in his army-cordoned palace, issued daily statements blaming the rebels. The single issue they seemed to agree on was to leave the hotels alone. Elsewhere terror continued unabated.

Hidden deep in the tangled maze of dark twisting streets that compose the Moslem quarter lived Saeb Salam. From his palatial home, rising like a cathedral above the mud and tarpaper shacks smeared along surrounding streets of this old Arab section, Salam commanded the rebellion. His was the voice of the Opposition. His word was law to hundreds of rebel fighters and terrorists.

Saeb Salam rarely left his home those days. On his order the entire Moslem quarter was barricaded. No one in, no one out, except by Salam's approval. Not even city garbage collectors dared defy the rebel cordon, so filth and disease mounted. In fact, the only people who could safely crash those barricades were foreign correspondents. True to the international brotherhood of rebel leaders, Salam was not publicity shy. Any visitor with a notebook in hand was welcome.

So we decided to pay a call.

If finding the Minotaur in the labyrinth of Knossos was tedious, this was downright discomposing. Establishing phone contact with Salam's headquarters in the first place was enough to deter the stoutest heart. The government had installed a scrambler on his telephone which made any conversation of over three words impossible. It took Welles twelve separate calls to convey our simple request to visit, and then a few more to hear the positive reply. A man named Sami was to be our contact, we were informed. Within half an hour he presented himself at the hotel to complete the arrangements.

Anyone unaccustomed to meeting rebel contact men rather expects the Peter Lorre type: furtive glances, coat collar high, unshaven. Sami had all of these, but on him they only looked silly; for Sami was a gawky boy of fifteen whose unshaven look could have been licked off by a kitten. He was well versed in the correct mannerisms, however, and by the time we completed our arrangements, we too were stealing glances over shoulders and fingering coat collars nervously. But he looked so like a drama student padding his part that we couldn't help but smile when he crept warily away.

We were to rendezvous with Sami at five-thirty that afternoon in the lobby of a fourth-rate downtown hotel. From there he would lead us into the bowels of the Basta, the Moslem quarter where Salam waited. So half an hour in advance we hailed a taxi and left the hotel.

Up through familiar streets we sped, those climbing narrow lanes leading from waterfront to town that we had come to know so well. The groundfloor shops bore two or three stories of apartments on their backs and, with blinds drawn against the street, seemed to be closing their eyes in grimaces protesting the weight. Red geraniums leaned precariously from higher window ledges. Now and again we glimpsed a frightened face peering from behind a curtained window. Few people were in the streets.

On our way to the Basta, Welles wanted to drive through the center of town and cross Place des Canons, the commercial section which had suffered most heavily from bomb attacks. Just to check. No incidents had been reported there this day so we felt little trepidation in approaching.

The square was quiet as we swung into it. It is a paved rectangular area, three blocks long by one wide, with a strip of plane trees in the center. In more peaceful days cars nose in among the trees while their owners visit the coffee shops and theaters that crowd each other around the square. But there were few cars or owners today. As we drove slowly up the first block of the perimeter, we should have recognized the threat of that calm.

We were halfway through the Square when the first shots came. We heard a guttural shout. From a small cafe on the far corner, seven men ran crazed with fright into the street. Three fell in the volley of shots that followed.

With that, the whole square erupted in gunfire, and I hit the floor in the back seat of the car as our driver braked to a curb. My nose was pressed into the carpet, and Welles doubled himself over me for protection. But he kept his head up, just high enough to watch without being seen. Snipers fired down into the street from windows that had stared blankly moments before. Police moved in from the corners, ducking behind boarded kiosks, aiming, firing, stalking on. One gunman used a parked taxi as his shield until a grenade demolished it, silencing his gun in a shower of leaves from the trees overhead. Another grenade blasted inside the corner cafe, raining window-glass fragments over the street. A few more scattered shots and it was done. Quiet again. The quiet of death for some thirty victims sprawled in the streets.

The tumult lasted only about five minutes, but from my vantage point it seemed more like an hour. A terrifying one at that. I was reminded of one Fourth of July when I was a child when I had somehow been trapped in the middle of a sandbox surrounded by exploding fireworks: no way to escape, wordlessly praying to be spared, terrified but helpless. But emerging undamaged then as now.

Our driver needed no urging to start up again and leave that turmoil. He eased his taxi through the stunned crowd as Welles and I untangled ourselves, but abruptly he stopped again. A gaunt, stern man had jumped right in front of the car, refusing to let us pass. Then he darted around to my side, forced open the door, and pushed in a ragged barefoot boy. Jabbering Arabic, the man slammed the door and waved us frantically forward.

"His father was just killed," murmured our driver, gesturing toward the child. "The boy saw it all. The man asks if we will take him home."

"Of course," Welles said softly, and I felt a golfball growing in my throat.

He was a small boy, probably about eight years old, with a pinched hungry look and wrists so thin I could have circled them both with my forefinger and thumb. His frayed brown jacket was patched and the shoulder seams hung nearly to his elbows. I guessed that it had been his father's.

Just then another burst of gunfire rang through the street behind us. I dived for the floorboards, pulling the child down with me. But he shrugged free and sat back stiff and straight as a ramrod on the seat, without a flicker of emotion on his face.

"Malish," he said, spitting out the word sharply. Then again, with drawn-out emphasis: "Ma-*lish!*" Thus he disposed of life, death, war, world, today, tomorrow. That Arabic word meaning "it doesn't matter" was his epitaph to this day of horror. In one afternoon he became older than any of us.

It was hard to continue our journey after we took the boy home. This was a Moslem child whose father had been killed by Moslems. So what kind of war was it, after all? Had the father been pro-government? Or had he merely wanted a cup of coffee at the wrong time? Or is that the essence of war anyway: man, wrong time, wrong place, dead. My desire to visit Saeb Salam paled to the point of extinction.

But on we went. Sami was waiting at the hotel as scheduled, joined us in the car, and directed us on to the Minotaur.

Sami was our passport through the rubbish-filled Basta streets. After we passed the entrance to the Moslem quarter, there were gunmen everywhere. Lounging against mud walls, rifles propped against stones. Squatting on curbs beside gutters swimming with orange peels and cigarette stubs. Some at attention on street corners. Others kneeling over cooking braziers. All unshaven and dirty. All with guns. They looked at us with alarm, but the sight of Sami brought salutes and a return to idleness.

Finally we came to a barbed-wire barrier blocking the street; a deep trough had been shoveled out of the paving behind it stretching the width of the street. It was there we parked as Sami explained that now we would have to walk.

Picking our way through litters of debris and garbage, around stone barricades, across narrow planks spanning booby-trap street pits, past curious ragged people of the neighborhood, eventually we were in front of Salam's home.

It was a three-story orange stucco mansion protected from street noise by a deep arbored garden through which a cobble path led to the door. Nearing the house, we saw that war had been here too, for the facing was pockmarked with mortar wounds. This, then, was the reason for barricades and guards: Salam did not wish to be found again.

We were searched upon entering. Or rather, Welles was. I watched as his slim six-foot frame was patted up and down in a check for concealed weapons, and decided right then that if anyone tried to frisk *me* I would start stoning. But when the guard turned toward me, Welles stopped him with a wave, so we were bowed into the elevator and conveyed to the "Presence."

The evil Saeb-Bey turned out to be no more frightening than the stereotype Tammany politician: booming, back-slapping, cigar-smoking. A dark stocky man with florid complexion, balding head, and a wide smile that was too constant to be altogether sincere. He greeted us warmly when we stepped from the elevator into his third-floor living room. A jovial quip, an effusive handshake, and a clap on the shoulder. I thought of the little boy again and shuddered.

Welles and Saeb Salam began talking about the revolution as soon as we were seated. I listened as closely as possible but my attention was caught by the huge stacks of guns around the room. Some were piled high on a Louis Quinze table; others lay beside a delicate porcelain tea service. The transition from gracious home to armed headquarters showed clearly. We drank thick Turkish coffee in tiny Dresden cups while Saeb-Bey loudly disclaimed responsibility for the terrorism in town. At the windows, grizzled gunmen shifted their feet and smiled self-consciously.

Then from a door at the rear of the room, a small woman

27

came quietly to join us. Welles stood up to greet her, and his broad-shouldered height made her seem fragile by comparison. She was dressed in a blue cotton dress and matching sweater with flat shoes. I was struck by the gentleness of her face and her smile which was almost shy.

This was Mrs. Salam, the woman who had been living for weeks hidden behind rebel barricades but who looked as if she had just returned from a picnic. Behind her came three small dark replicas of Salam, boys ranging in age from about five to twelve, who bowed low before us and shook hands in the best Oxford manner. My picture of rebels tilted at this and I felt that someone had switched casts on us in the middle of the play. Only later, when Welles explained that Salam was once Lebanon's prime minister and his wife a community leader and the product of French schools, could I finally sort out the discrepancies.

Lebanese tradition reserves the post of president of the republic for Maronite Catholics and that of prime minister for Sunni Moslems, a system of communal checks and balances. This had long proved a successful working arrangement, which in essence was the tragedy of the present rebellion: Moslem leaders like Salam were manipulating religious antagonisms to oust a president whom they considered too pro-West. They wanted Lebanon aligned with Egypt's Nasser instead, in a move toward Arab nationalism. It is generally believed that Nasser actually directed the Lebanese revolution from Cairo. In any case, the rebels were always welcome at the Egyptian Embassy in Beirut those days. Welles found Salam henchmen slipping out of the ambassador's office whenever he called there.

But whatever their political convictions, both sides were stirring up religious fervor in moves calculated to create chaos. This was the true horror of Lebanon, 1958.

Yet here we were, sitting with the leader of rebel fanaticism, listening to his ideas about revolution. Our own opinions did not count, except as Welles used his for provoking discussion. Salam had to be understood if we were to report the revolution objectively. When Mrs. Salam invited us to stay for dinner, it seemed that understanding was near.

28

She led the way into the dining room where about a dozen of Salam's fighters were already seated and eating ravenously. They hardly looked up. We took our places and were helping ourselves from the cold platters and bowls of Arab specialties when the dining-room door flew open and two gunmen stamped in, out of breath, hiding rifles awkwardly behind them. Salam's polite smile froze, his eyes hardening. Clearly these men were not invited.

Salam's chair scraped roughly as he jumped from the table, shoved the two back out the door, and, following them, slammed it behind him. Mrs. Salam tried to cover his abrupt departure with conversation, and Welles kindly helped her out. But I found that I was having a little trouble swallowing at the moment and I couldn't take my eyes off that door.

He returned minutes later, stiff and nervous.

"A few men were hurt in a skirmish outside," Salam murmured. "Nothing serious but we must care for them. So perhaps it might be wise if you leave soon. There might be more fighting."

"I *am* sorry," Mrs. Salam said as we left the room together. "I had hoped that we would have time to really talk. The only people I see anymore are fighters. My biggest job is trying to keep cheerful," she confided. "But sometimes smiling is hard."

I don't know what it was. Certainly not the rebel cause. But suddenly my heart went out to her and I slipped a silver bracelet from my wrist onto hers. She put an arm around her husband's waist and, with a slight lift of her chin, smiled her thanks. The love and trust in that simple gesture explained everything. For in spite of her difficulties, Mrs. Salam did indeed smile.

Sami was waiting on the ground floor to guide us out. Now it was black moonless night, the street deserted and silent. Stopping us with a gesture at the door, he went ahead to the garden gate, cupped a hand to his mouth, and whistled a low "whoo-oo-ee" into the stillness. A moment later, like an echo from the black street, came an answering whistle.

"All right," Sami whispered. "Our night guards on the roofs expect us. They won't shoot."

If this was supposed to calm us, it certainly missed. In pitch-darkness we stumbled back toward our car, over booby traps, around the barricades, accompanied by low whistles which bounced from roof to roof as Basta guards alerted one another to our presence and passed us along with approval. Knowing that we were closely watched by so many hidden eyes was nerve-wracking, but we took comfort in the certainty that on that evening, anyway, no thug of Salam's would dare kill a journalist!

5

The Devil's Sandbox

Mondays are rather dismal, I think. It is probably a conditioned reflex from my working days, but somehow I have never been able to muster up any enthusiasm for starting a bright new week. It is usually sometime Tuesday afternoon before I finally get into the spirit of the thing.

Welles, on the other hand, is a fast starter. He wakes easily in the morning, without the several cups of coffee I require. He is able to carry on intelligent telephone conversations before breakfast, and occasionally he even broadcasts. New weeks for him are things of beauty, surely filled with excitement and adventure.

We do not, therefore, exactly see eye to eye on Mondays.

So it was with a decided yearning to return to the warmth of my bed that I heard him sing out one morning: "Well dear, it's Monday, July fourteenth. I wonder what this week will bring."

I was thankful later that we sat down to a relaxed breakfast that morning, because it was the last relaxed sitting we were to do all week. Welles left the hotel right after breakfast on the usual round of checking for news developments. I carried my coffee cup and the morning papers out to the "forbidden" balcony overlooking the sea, and had just settled down to a peaceful half hour of leisurely awakening when the door flew open and he raced back into the room.

"Hi, dear," I called through a yawn. "That was a short day. Or did you forget something?"

"I'm afraid that it will be a very long day, baby," he said, his voice coming indistinctly from the room. I could hear dresser drawers opening and then slamming, papers being shuffled, and a few unintelligible words that sounded like "Iraq" and "revolution." It was exactly enough to bring me flying into the room, which was being torn apart by my wild-eyed husband.

"Looking for passports," he muttered, "and money. How much do you have? Traveler's checks! Where are all of our traveler's checks?"

I started for the desk to find our passports, switched course to get my purse, changed my mind and headed for the locked suitcase containing our traveler's checks, then halted abruptly. We were darting around the room like a couple of minnows in search of a school. Getting nowhere except in each other's way.

"Hey, wait a minute!" I said. "What *is* this? What's happened?"

"Revolution in Iraq . . . middle of the night . . . palace overthrown," he mumbled, continuing his frantic search. "King probably killed . . . army revolt . . . tourists murdered in a hotel . . . probably some Americans. . . ."

He was on his knees with his face in a desk drawer by this time and suddenly, with an exclamation of delight, he stood up waving our passports in the air.

"Great! I found them!" Welles beamed. "I'll go book us seats on the next plane to Baghdad. Leaves in two hours." And he rushed out, slammed the door, and was gone.

Fun's fun, I thought, but this is ridiculous! Who on God's green earth would deliberately choose to go to such a place? Then I headed slowly for the bathroom and turned on a cold cold shower. For the answer was obvious: *we* would.

The trouble with me is that I grew up with an older brother. He is two years older than I, and the fact that we are great friends today attests admirably to his indulgence. My first twelve years were lived in an agony of trying to please and I trailed along behind him and his friends, rapt in the wondrous things they could do. I would be ignored totally for days, silently but happily watching the boys build a new scooter or treehouse or death-defying midget skyway. And then the glorious moment would come when they amply repaid my devotion by allowing me to be the first to try their invention. Danger? What is that to a little girl, compared to the ecstasy of being accepted by her big brother as a member, however expendable, of the gang?

To be the wife of a foreign correspondent, only girls with older brothers need apply. With such training, the time for decision never arises. I could no more think of refusing to accompany Welles on such a trip than I could have stayed off that death-defying midget skyway. But . . . did it have to be *Baghdad?*

I was dressed in my black linen traveling suit, had our bags packed, and was halfway through what I suspected might well be my last letter to my parents, when Welles returned. One glance at his face made me forget all of my trepidations in a rush of pity, for I had never seen him look so dejected.

"The Baghdad airport is closed," he said dolefully, "so the airline can't fly in. I had us reserved on the flight too. Rotten luck."

"Maybe there is another way," I offered brightly. Once I have decided to leap into a frying pan, I hate to be netted in mid-air.

"I thought of chartering a plane," he countered, "but the companies are afraid to try it now that the airport is closed. Afraid that they might get shot down."

I thought that the charter companies showed a remarkable degree of perception, and sighed rather too audibly with relief.

"Maybe we could fly to another city in Iraq," I suggested. "Is the airport at Basra still open?"

Welles brightened considerably and I even got a kiss for my brilliance. A minute later we were on our way to an airlines office which we knew had a thick international book listing flight schedules. I found that it also had a huge blue-and-green map of the Middle East covering one whole wall, with bright red flight routes superimposed. With my limited knowledge of geography, I stationed myself before it while Welles consulted the reservations clerk.

As I studied the map I could hear them solemnly dismissing

cities one after the other. Basra and Mosul were discarded because no airline would hazard landing anywhere inside Iraq now. No point in flying to Amman because the Jordanian-Iraqi border had just closed. Teheran? No flights from Beirut today, and the ensuing drive from Teheran to Baghdad would be too arduous anyway.

"Is there a flight to Kuwait?" I inquired, wondering at my own tenacity. Would I *never* learn to quit while still ahead? My map showed Kuwait as a pinpoint on the Persian Gulf, just south of Iraq. It looked like a mere stroll from there to the border.

"There is," said the clerk, regarding us more quizzically than ever. "You can leave at one A.M. on Air Liban and, with the time change, be there at six in the morning."

Welles and I hugged each other with delight, and our friend shook his head sorrowfully. I had the feeling that he had been playing where's-the-thimble with us all along, knowing about Kuwait but benevolently hoping that we would recover our senses before *we* found it.

Tickets finally in hand, we hurried off to the Iraqi Embassy to obtain visas. There utter confusion reigned: consuls didn't know whether King Feisal was alive or dead, whether there was a government at all, whether they in fact were still consuls. Even the gold-framed portrait of Feisal that commanded the room seemed to have an uncertain smile as he gazed bleakly down on us from the wall. The tight-lipped Iraqi woman who gave us our visas was a Lady Macbeth whose eyes were open but their sense shut. The place was heavy with infectious dread and we quit it abruptly before we too should be contaminated.

Apparently there are very few people in the world who wish to fly to Kuwait in the middle of the night. We were sitting in almost solitary splendor on our DC-6 that night, and as we belted the seat straps across our laps the thought struck me that the rest of the world's people must know something that we did not and that we were rushing headlong into a fate others had shunned. Nonetheless, we were excited and eager to get on with it. Welles had completed a series of broadcasts in the afternoon and I had sent off my parents' letter, so we were leaving all strings tied neatly. I tucked my hand in Welles' and gave him what I hoped was a confident smile, but the intense pall of fear that had clouded the Iraqi Embassy that morning lingered with me. The memory was hard to shake.

It was nearly six o'clock when our plane began its descent over the flat barren waste that is Kuwait. The desert looked endless in the early morning sun and the lusterless waters of the Persian Gulf reflected a harsh glare in air already heavy with heat.

If there is a hotter, drier place on earth than Kuwait in mid-July, I hope never to find it. We stepped out of our cool airplane straight into a bake-oven. By the time we had cleared customs and immigration, we could have been planked and labeled "well done." Our faces were flushed and damp, and my suit was as crisp as a withered petunia. As additional discomfort, we found the airport teeming with alarmed Kuwaitis who were fighting for seats on outgoing planes, fearful that the violence in Iraq would spread across the border and endanger them. Getting through that surging mob was like trying to go the wrong way in a revolving door; once again we seemed to be hurrying toward what everyone else was hurrying from. But I thought of lemmings and followed Welles downstream out to the street.

The Kuwait we saw that day was a totally undistinguished little town composed of two-story clay buildings lumped along arid sand streets. Its one paved main street was locked tailfin-to-bumper with ostentatious American cars ineptly maneuvered by swarthy Arabs. Their traditional kaffiyeh headdress restricted their side vision sufficiently to make every intersection a hazard. The sheikhs had no way then to spend their wealth except on new cars, but there was no place to drive to so they simply steered up and down the main street all day, proudly bumping into each other. Since then, oil revenues have been put to more beneficent uses in a frenzy of construction. Kuwait has good public housing now, broad avenues, and the most modern university complex in the world. Improvement programs had been started even then to raise living standards, but the Kuwait we saw was a tarnished carnival concession whose automobiles crashed and crumpled noisily in a stifling arena of sand and grit.

Our Kuwait mentor, the American consul, Talcott Seelye, did not hide the fact that he considered us out of our minds to attempt the drive to Iraq. With real anxiety he informed us that he had been unable to contact any American in Baghdad or Basra since the coup the day before. All official information channels had been severed and he had no more idea of the true state of things in Iraq than we. He thought that the border might still be open, but cautioned us to take sufficient food and water for the trip.

"Once you leave Kuwait, you won't see another human being until the border," Seelye advised dourly. "It is a tough trip, just desert. There is no road at all, literally, so be sure that your driver is dependable."

What I had thought would be an easy, short drive to the border in fact was to be four hours of absolute hell in the torrid wastes. But as we rattled off and struck out across the empty desert, jolting and bouncing over pathless dunes, our faces seared by hot sandy wind, we laughed and chattered like children. Our goal was within reach and we were drunk with exhilarating confidence.

That afternoon as the shadows lengthened over the desert and heat rose from the baked sands, we were back again in those dunes. This time jolting in the opposite direction. This time trailed by outriding Iraq Army jeeps loaded with armed guards. This time silent, dejected as whipped puppies. Our great gamble had lost; we were barred from entering Iraq.

The real ache in our disappointment was that our gamble almost worked. Iraqi border guards at Safwan treated us like visiting royalty when we first arrived and put us through the familiar Coke-coffee-Seven-up routine. Their obsequiousness was nauseating, but we had to do it their way. This Alfonse-Gaston charade was played out in the army captain's office where the pungency of dung cooking-fuel, fused with tobacco fumes, made smiling difficult. Just as our visas were about to be stamped, which would have allowed us to proceed to Baghdad, a phone call came from the army commander in Basra and smiles were no longer needed. Not only were we refused admission to Iraq, we were ordered to return to Kuwait posthaste under heavy armed guard. The day of royalty, visiting or otherwise, was dead. Even my half-empty Coke bottle was snatched away, along with our long-sought goal.

At least Welles got the story. During the three hours we spent in that impoverished border village, arguing and pleading to be permitted to continue on to Baghdad, the picture became clear: the coup was indeed nationwide. The army was in tight control, with a clique of officers acting as dictator. King Feisal and his prime minister, Nuri es-Said, had been murdered. And the borders were sealed against all transit of people or communications. We were not even allowed to phone American Consul David Scott in Basra because the army also controlled all telephone lines.

Our spirits could not have been lower as we drove back to Kuwait. That is, we didn't *think* they could, which was some solace. But once again we were wrong. The mortal blow to our journalist hearts was leveled by the American consul to whom we returned in defeat.

He met us ashen-faced at the consulate door and pronounced benediction: "The American Marines have just landed in Beirut."

It was the biggest story of all, and we weren't there.

6

Black Tuesday

As we were bouncing hopefully over the Kuwait desert toward Iraq that day before the axe fell, in Beirut another American journalist had embarked on a tenacity jag of his own. It was John Law of *U.S. News and World Report,* trying to get to Baghdad *his* way.

"Look!" John exploded to the mincing airlines clerk at Beirut airport. "I've got to get on that plane to Amman! I don't believe there is a waiting list and furthermore even if there is one a mile long, you get me on that plane!"

John glared down at the clerk from his six-foot-six advantage and said, "The plane I want leaves in an hour. I'll be back in thirty minutes to pick up my ticket." And he stamped out of the airport waiting room to get some air on the observation deck above.

Grumbling to himself about the lack of acumen of airlines clerks, John grappled with his temper and wandered to the edge of the deck overlooking the field. He had already been at the airport for several hours trying to get to Iraq, and had long since wearied of reports that airports were closing and planes were being grounded. Having reached the decision to try the Amman route and to attempt to crash the Iraqi border by car, he had exhausted his patience and was determined to get-the-hell-out.

"Must get to Baghdad," he growled to himself. "Nothing happening here in Beirut, and look at me: trapped! But at least I'll get to Amman."

John looked out over the glistening tarmac and took a deep breath to calm himself. Then he stopped dead. He shook his head, blinked his eyes, and looked again.

"By God," he muttered faintly. "By good God, it's the Marines!"

His fingers tugged an earlobe for a minute while he strained his eyes to be sure. Yes, there they were: honest-to-goodness United States Marines, landing in green helicopters all over the Beirut airport. Then John cleared the stairs down from the deck in two leaps, waved off the airlines clerk who tried to give him the Amman ticket, bolted out of the airport waiting-room door, and flagged a taxi for town. The Marines were landing in Lebanon, and that meant just one thing: American intervention. John Law had his story.

In the northern part of the Syrian desert another American foreign correspondent with a troubled but determined face fidgeted in the back seat of a taxi as it approached Damascus. The heat was exhausting and he felt little streams of sweat coursing down his chest and between his shoulder blades under his bush shirt. Joe Alex Morris, Jr., then writing for the New York *Herald Tribune,* had tried *his* hunch and lost.

"It would have been a good try anyway," Joe thought glumly. "If only this damn driver hadn't lost his nerve, we would almost be to the Iraqi border by now. I'll just have to get another and try again." And then, growling at the driver, he said for the tenth time, "But don't think I am going to pay *you* a damn penny!"

Joe slumped down in the seat and nursed his frustration all the way into Damascus.

When they pulled up in front of the taxi office, Joe flung himself out of the car and slammed the door on the protests of his driver. Marching up to a clerk inside, he demanded another taxi.

"I am going to Iraq," he shouted angrily, "and you are going to get me a driver who will take me! This bastard you gave me is afraid of his own shadow and I've lost half a day because of him!"

Bravely aware that three feet of solid counter separated him from his irate customer, the clerk said haughtily, "I am very sorry, sir. No driver will attempt the Iraq trip now. I suggest that you return to Beirut and take a plane from there."

Joe had long possessed a colorful vocabulary. This day he brought forth every expletive and invented a few extras on the spot. But an hour later, bitter and disheartened, he simmered down, hunched in the corner of a car taking him to Beirut. Sick with disappointment, Joe Morris knew that he had lost the Iraq story. But he couldn't know that directly ahead, over that last mountain, waited the biggest news of all . . . and that he would get there just in time.

There were many other correspondents treading water in this tidal wave. Some were submerged, some rode in on lucky rollers, and some got rolled in the surf and wound up with mouthfuls of sand.

Unhappily we were among the sand chewers. Having worked so hard to get to this never-never land called Kuwait, now suddenly we couldn't get out of it. The Beirut airport had closed down tight during the American landing and no one dared to guess when it might reopen. We discovered to our horror that the next flight from Kuwait *anywhere* was not until the next morning, and to Jerusalem at that.

"Well, what is the best hotel here?" Welles asked the gloomy American consul who distractedly cast nervous glances over his shoulder into the darkened consulate building. The electricity had just failed and the consul's wife, sure that it was sabotage and that they were about to be lynched by anti-American mobs, was wandering around in the gloom with candlesticks clutched in both hands like Tosca.

"The best is Ziggy's Hotel," our friend stuttered, his tongue on constant duty moistening tight gray lips. "If you don't mind a third-rate hotel, it really is the best."

We were glad to be off downtown then, because both the consul and his wife had such morbid jitters that we welcomed escaping to Ziggy's Hotel, third-rate or not. And besides, we heard that it was Swiss-owned and that usually means good lodging. But when we got our first glimpse of Ziggy's with its ramshackle three stories, peeling paint and sagging front stoop, we wondered what the consul would grade "fourth-rate" and shuddered.

It was grim. If the owner was indeed Swiss, he hadn't been home in a long time. The lobby was a dim cupboard hung with room keys which had number plaques so grotesque that guests not only ran no risk of forgetting them in pockets but could hardly carry them as far as their rooms. The hall was lit by one naked twenty-five-watt bulb that hung from a long ceiling cord and was clouded by a swarm of mesmerized gnats. Faded flowered wallpaper clung in places to the walls, and the carpet emitted such a puff of dust when we stepped to the reception desk that I exploded in a fit of sneezing.

The brightest bit of news all day was that Ziggy's Hotel also had an annex. Sight unseen we figured that the annex could not be worse than this, so Welles registered us in room 1-A (for Annex) and we picked up our bags and prepared to investigate. *Then* we learned that the annex was away across town and had no dining room. Dinner here in the hotel would be served only for another hour. In short, we could either eat or bathe; there was no time for both. And even a drink was out of the question because Kuwait is dry.

It would be a dismal decision at best, so I was prepared to let Welles do the coin-flipping, when a saint intervened. Neither of us had noticed the man who was observing our plight until he introduced himself at that moment. He was a European airline representative who had the coarse luck of being stationed in Kuwait. And it developed that he was so thoroughly in the doghouse with his guardian angel that he was *living* in Ziggy's Hotel.

"Here, wait," he interrupted, lumbering over to the desk. "You two look as though you have about had it. I have a room here, just upstairs. It isn't much, but it has hot water and a bottle of scotch. You look like you need both pretty bad," he grinned. "So get on up there and I'll see you later."

Have you ever seen a man turn to gold? Pure, lustrous, glit-

41

tering 24-carat gold? I saw one right then, complete with halo. Welles thanked him with the desperate gratitude we both felt, and we groped blindly down the dim hall to the staircase leading to our benefactor's room.

It wasn't the kind of bathroom you will ever see in an advertisement, but the little cubbyhole we found off the bedroom looked beautiful. It was about six feet long by two wide, half of which was a stall shower minus curtain. And it had an endless supply of steaming hot water which was like the balm of absolution as it streamed through my hair, into my smarting eyes and over all my aching muscles and nerves.

"Oh honey, just wait!" I called happily, drying myself off. "It is divine! Makes you feel like a new person."

"I *am* just waiting," Welles grumbled as he handed me a tall scotch. "And for a long time too. What were you doing in there anyway? Playing with boats?"

It is no fun at all to lose a story, and losing two of the biggest stories in the world on the same day is about as demoralizing for a newsman as anything could be. It was discouraging for me but profoundly so for Welles, yet I heard neither complaints nor self-pity. He had done his best, and failed. There was nothing more to be said.

I realized then that this was a dimension of his character I had not fully appreciated before: Welles simply did not know the *meaning* of self-pity. In this sense, our Black Tuesday in Kuwait was a revelation. And I think that I loved him more in that moment than I ever had before. It was a feeling that even zymotic Ziggy's could not dim.

Slipping back into our damp, sandy clothes was not pleasant, but we had another cold scotch and felt ready for anything. Anything, that is, except the scene that awaited us in the dining room.

It was just like walking on stage in the midst of Eugene O'Neill's *The Iceman Cometh*. There were six other principals onstage when we stepped through the dining-room door. As if on cue, they halted all motion and speech and watched us listlessly as we crossed the dingy room to our table. Two men sharing the table nearest us resumed their discourse as soon as we were seated; with elbows on the table, they noisily ladled consommé into their mouths while mumbling something that sounded like monosyllabic German, which is a feat in itself. To their left sat a grayed-out couple who did not speak at all but watched us covetously the whole time. At a third table in the corner was a dowdy middle-aged woman with a little boy who showed no trace of youth but instead sat dully pushing vegetables around his plate with a fork. It was the River Styx which flowed to our door. The room's atmosphere was cumbrous with weary acceptance. It was as if even Death had passed it by uncaring.

We ate little of the uninspired meal and spoke quietly so as not to disturb the pall. But our slight veneer of composure crumbled when our vapid fellow diners rose in a body and filed out of the room, each nodding to us in turn and murmuring "Good evening" in voices devoid of expression. Their unquestioning acceptance of us in their purgatory was the alarming thing. We skipped our after-dinner coffees and all but *ran* from the dining room, flagged a taxi, and headed for our Kuwait home-away-from-home-away-from-home: the Annex.

The beds were wire cots, but something to stretch out on anyway. And we were utterly exhausted, physically and emotionally, so we were asleep within minutes and did not take time to investigate our lodging. That was a blessing because the next morning at five o'clock, when we were awakened to prepare for our seven-thirty flight to Jerusalem, we saw quite enough.

I had left my suitcase open beside the bed the night before: mistake number one. As I dug into it that morning, a cockroach fully two inches long ambled out from beneath my robe. I tried to pretend that he was just another Archie in search of Mehitabel, but it didn't quite come off and I jumped up with a shout. Welles came back at that moment from showering in the adjoining room, and I screamed, "Look! *Do* something! He's a monster!"

My husband, loaded with early morning empathy, just laughed.

"If that little fellow bothers you," he advised brightly, "don't take a shower. His whole family lives under the shower floor-board and they gallop all over the place when it rains."

That was enough for me. Bathless I went to the airport with my indomitably clean husband. We boarded the plane for Jerusalem and neither of us gave Kuwait a backward glance.

Black Tuesday and its blacker night were behind us. I reached for Welles' hand and pulled it high in a boxer's victory sign. Because, after all, everything *is* relative.

7

The Philadelphia Blues

As long as I can remember, I have wanted to visit Jerusalem. Even though we were heading there only because it was a port in the storm, I was highly excited. But somewhere between Kuwait and Jerusalem, my good fairy must have bailed out of that airplane. For it looked as though the only thing that we would see this trip was the airport. Hot, stuffy, crowded Jerusalem airport, which is just like any other airport except that it has more flies.

"But why don't we take an hour or so to look around, now that we are here?" I said, trying to keep pace as Welles hurried through the terminal to the Beirut ticket counter. "I *know* that we are behind on the story and that we should get back. But for God's sake, honey, even *you* have to slow down sometime. A few hours can't really matter."

I might have been talking to the wall for all the good it did.

We were next in line at the counter now and time was running out. All right, I thought, if *you* want to fly straight on back to Beirut, go ahead! *I* am going to stay.

Then Welles turned and looked at me. It was a moment before he spoke.

"If you don't understand by now why I have to get back," he said, so coldly that it stung, "there is no point in my telling you." And he turned back to the ticket agent, leaving me rooted to the floor with shock.

I don't know what would have happened had there been a flight to Beirut right then, but there wasn't. Airports in Lebanon were still closed, so it was academic. And once again I felt a rush of compassion for my husband when I saw the frustration reflected in his face. Then I *did* understand: a newsman stays on a story until it's over. It's as simple as that. And I knew it too.

"Well, we had better claim our luggage," Welles said. "And then I'll try to think of something."

Off we went again across the terminal, past a newsstand, a coffee shop, and a bank of telephone booths. There Welles stopped abruptly, whirled, and headed for the nearest one.

"I think I have an idea," he said. "Wait here, if you will. I'll be with you in a minute." He stepped inside the phone booth and let the door slide shut.

When he emerged a few minutes later, his face was brighter than I had seen it in two days.

"I just phoned Dan in Amman," he said excitedly. "It is just a hunch but I think that it might pay off. Let's go on up there and see him."

Well, this was something anyway. Instead of climbing right back on another airplane and seeing nothing of the Holy Land, we would drive the three-hour stretch to Jordan's capital and pass Jericho, the Dead Sea, and the River Jordan. And then a reunion in Amman with our friends Dan and Elizabeth Brown, the American press attaché in Jordan and his wife. I was so pleased that I forgot to ask why Welles had decided on Amman.

His hunch was excellent, as it turned out. Winston Churchill created Jordan at the end of World War I and ever since, the British have considered that rocky little kingdom well within their area of influence. Even the rugged Arab Legion, Jordan's proud army, had been organized and commanded by the British general John Bagot Glubb. And although overt display of British military interest ceased with Glubb's ouster in 1956, the 1948 treaty of mutual assistance remained in force. So now, with Jordan's eastern neighbor Iraq in the throes of revolution and with the U.S. Sixth Fleet landing on the nearby Mediterranean coast, would it not be reasonable to suppose that the British might fly troops into Amman to bolster Jordan's independence?

46

It was. And we were there when it happened.

My prescient husband explained all this to me as we wound through the brown hills of Judea that morning, leaving Jerusalem for Amman with only a hunch to guide us. I knew that it would be important later for me to understand the situation, but right then our road made current events seem ludicrous. It wound away from Jerusalem's ancient stone walls whose seventeenth-century parapets still contemplate the issues of human inequity. Then along the foot of the Mount of Olives, past the green Garden of Gethsemane where Jesus knew solitude and the agony of man. It was difficult to be concerned over modern foibles when my head was swiveling like that of a tennis umpire as I tried to capture glimpses of those consecrated sites.

"Quite a feeling, isn't it?" Welles said quietly. "Why don't we plan to come back in a few days after we check on Amman? Would you like that?"

I shook my head in wonder. He was telling me that he not only understood my outburst, but also that he knew I had understood his. What do you *do* with a man like this! Simply love him.

I forgot that the Hangen timetable suffers from chronic delays and obstructions imposed by Middle Eastern caprice. Once again, the few days we anticipated were to stretch endlessly on. Little Jordan was on the brink of upheaval and we would remain in her capital city nearly a month, until she was led safely back from the fissure's edge.

But our drive from Jerusalem to Amman that day was fascinating, in spite of 100-degree heat and a narrow road that winds through steep, barren cliffs. For it is impossible to travel that twisting route without envisioning the trials of Jesus and his disciples as they trod the same path for the last time from Jericho to Jerusalem; impossible to cross the lazy Jordan River at its ancient, narrow ford without remembering Joshua; impossible to shy away from Dead Sea waters crusted with the engulfed evil of Sodom and Gomorrah, to gaze up at bleak Mt. Nebo, to pass brittle white Christ-thorn bushes, without being awed by our heritage.

And then, too soon, we came to the hilly beige bowl that is Amman.

Actually Jordan's capital is no city at all but rather a succession of dusty hills covered with clinging clay dwellings. Snaking between the hills is a deep gully that wanders like a child's sand trail. The mercantile and produce stores lining this paved stream-bed distinguish it as Amman's main street. It is a city devoid of color, except for the red-checkered kaffiyehs worn by Arab legionnaires. There are few trees or flowers.

But Amman does have a rambling hotel of somewhat tarnished splendor called the Philadelphia. It faces a well-preserved Roman amphitheater and is a fairly comfortable haven.

As we swung into the circle drive fronting the hotel, terrace tea-drinkers put down their cups and watched our arrival with open curiosity. We were among the first of the mass of journalists soon to descend on Amman, and these entrenched Philadelphians viewed us with suspicion, jealous of their peace.

Tired, and a bit unsettled by our stony reception, I said (too loudly) to Welles, "It looks nice, honey, but why in the world would they name a hotel Philadelphia way over here in Jordan?"

That was all we needed to make our grand entrance complete. I learned later that Philadelphia was Amman's Greek name in the second century before Christ and that we, and William Penn, were the borrowers. I decided right then to study ancient history, and quickly.

We were in luck. The concierge announced beneficently that he had an air-conditioned room we could have. He let us know that since only a few rooms were so honored, he was doing us a magnificent favor and expected to be fondly remembered. It was almost dusk and the thermometer still clung somewhere near 90 degrees, so we ascended by ancient, groaning elevator to our third-floor room, eager to bask in cool seclusion. If anything, our room was even hotter than the air outside. We searched frantically for the air control panel, thinking someone had forgotten to turn on our glacial blasts.

"Slow down," Welles said finally, glaring into a corner. "Here's your famous air-conditioner." And he pointed contemptuously at an object hidden from my view, on a table. Dodging around him, I saw the saddest, oldest, rustiest little fan imaginable. It leaned wearily to one side like a small green tower of Pisa, with chipped enamel and three bent blades.

"Oh well, let's plug it in anyway," I sighed. "Maybe it's a zephyr in disguise." If so, the disguise was perfect; for when the cord was attached to the wall socket, it was worse. The motor wheezed, sputtered, and then worked its way up to a rattle. I pushed the blades a couple of times to give it the idea, but it demanded its own pace or nothing. For a time we expected nothing, but then it shuddered slightly, coughed, and started to churn. To our intense amazement it even found the will to rotate. We were in business! We might not get much conditioning, but at least we had a breath of air.

Welles scheduled a broadcast for ten o'clock that night and rushed off to meet Dan Brown at the American Embassy and confirm his hunch by getting latest developments. I stayed behind to unpack, hoping that none of our six-legged Kuwait friends had come along for the ride. None had, so I hung up a few things, formed a giant laundry parcel of the rest, and then relaxed in an easy chair at the window beside our little green groaner and admired the flowered patio below. How fortunate we were to have a room in the rear of the hotel overlooking such a quiet spot.

Welles returned shortly, excited by his news haul. In spite of jealous guarding by the British, Welles had the word that their planes would begin to land parachute troops the next morning. It was big news and we were far too stimulated to be hungry, so we ordered sandwiches in our room while Welles worked on his scripts.

Later, as he was pounding the typewriter in deep concentration, we began to hear discordant squeaks and squawks from the patio below.

"What on earth is *that?*" Welles asked, looking up from his work with a frown.

"Sounds like an orchestra tuning up," I murmured, peering into the patio in preference to watching the storm clouds I knew were gathering in our room. It was.

"A *what!*" he roared. And just then the strains of "I Don't Want to Set the World on Fire" came crashing up to our windows. It sounded like a flock of mating saxophones.

"Well, close the windows at least," he pleaded. "I can't think!" And he went back to his typing, mumbling "Orchestra!" darkly under his breath. I closed the windows. We couldn't breathe.

"Hot as hell in here," my beloved husband muttered, desperately trying to hang on to his train of thought. "Can't you open the windows?" I opened the windows. The orchestra launched into a brassy "Deep Purple" that pulsated in our room like an untuned calliope.

Welles jumped up, tore the unfinished script from his typewriter, put on his jacket and announced that he would finish at the broadcasting studio. And he left me beating time with irritable fingers on the arm of my chair.

Long before Welles returned I had devised a system to insulate us from our deafening neighbors that even Rube Goldberg would have approved. The fan, perched on a window ledge, wheezed and rattled noisily enough to drown out a couple of saxophones all by itself while stirring up the maximum of air. My chair sat on the opposite side of the room to the immediate right of a table radio turned to the Voice of America. With a plug in my right ear, my left ear nestled against the radio which played *modern* music, and my eyes focused on *The Bible as History* (which I bought from the concierge right after my Philadelphia gaffe), I am proud to report that I could not hear a single note from Roseland downstairs. I didn't even hear my husband when he entered the room, nor the whoop of laughter with which he approved my genius.

"Pull up a chair, dear," I said, when he shook me out of my cocoon. "The static is fine." And he joined me for a hiccuping

50

news broadcast before the Voice of America went off the air. We headed for bed to the thudding beat of "Roll Out the Barrel," and proved that it is possible to sleep like pillow sandwiches deep under the sheet and still live.

8

A Bus Named Liverpool

Welles was at Amman airport the next morning when the first hulking Beverly transport taxied up the runway. Its engines cut off and its four propellers slowed with rhythmic deliberation as if defying any fervent Arab nationalist to question its landing rights. The R.A.F. red bull's-eye flag reflecting on the plane's silver nose cast precise circular patterns on tarmac glistening from the heat. Even the tire skid marks looked more definitive than usual. There was no doubt that the British had come again to stay.

The last time British boots stamped this soil they were hurriedly retreating before the fury of Jordanian mobs after King Hussein had been forced to dismiss his trusted British commander, Lieutenant General John Bagot Glubb, in a bid for domestic popularity. More than half of Jordan's population is Palestinian, including over a half-million homeless refugees, who are lastingly bitter toward the British for the loss of their property in what is now Israel. Jordan had succumbed to nationalist fever; the "imperialist dogs" were repudiated. Therefore, it was with some trepidation that Hussein summoned the Lion again to his land. And it was a reticent Lion answering the call, since he could see both trees and forest in this Arab jungle: Hostile Jordanians would scream "aggression," an enraged Iraq would expect invasion, and the entire Arab world would condemn the "colonialists" for renewed encroachment upon its freedom. The troops did not know what to expect and so appeared staunchly ready for anything.

52

The United States Marines had experienced the same sort of uncertainty three days earlier when they landed in Beirut, but that, as it turned out, was something of a farcical disaster. Proud products of arduous training, the Marines waded through the Mediterranean's tumbling surf fully prepared to liberate a military objective. With full field packs and guns which were carried high above salt spray, they splashed ashore. Then the brave military demeanor gave way to perplexity. How does one go about liberating a place when its beaches are so crowded with sunbathers that they look impenetrable? Like Little Eva on the ice floe, the Marines vaulted bikini-clad ladies and children with sandpails by planting their boots in the sand cracks between them. And when they finally made it up the beach to the road, they found nothing more hostile than a bunch of aging pistachio vendors.

While these beached Marines were regrouping in confusion, other American troops were landing in helicopters at Beirut airport. Objective: secure the airport until Lebanese government troops could arrive to take over.

The only trouble was that government troops had already arrived and *had* taken over. It was only by a very narrow squeak that the gallant U.S. Marines did not stumble into a full-scale battle with their own paper allies. In fact, it took the siren-heralded appearance of U.S. Ambassador Robert McClintock with Lebanese Army General Chehab to clear the airport air and convince all hands that they were on the same side in this shooting match, and that there was not a rebel in sight.

Now, in Amman just three days later, it was anybody's guess as to what the British might be facing as the airplane doors swung open and their first troops returned to Jordan.

These were paratroopers, Her Majesty's proud "Red Devils." They sprang to the baked concrete runway with imperious clipped gait, their bearing straight in spite of full shoulder packs. The glint of well-oiled guns caught the sun and shot prisms of light along the tarmac. On each head rode a jaunty red beret, their badge of glory.

Welles was impressed by their authoritative manner. Here

were men who had come to do a job, no monkey business about it. A bit alarming in fact because they seemed almost like automatons. Slightly more than human, and yet slightly less. But then, a moment later, their humanity was delightfully affirmed. The first act performed on Jordanian soil by the ferocious Red Devils was to drop in their tracks beside the plane and—make tea!

"What language do they speak in this country?" asked a rosy-faced major, ambling over to Welles with a teacup in hand. Behind him, his squadron knelt around a camp stove set up on the runway. The tea kettle whistled and more cups were brewed.

Welles told him that Arabic is spoken in Jordan as well as in most other Middle Eastern countries.

"Odd, that," the officer commented with a frown. "I say, is it beastly difficult to learn? Or do you suppose they understand English too?"

Welles glanced around at all those glistening guns, and assured the major that his men would be understood even if they spoke Pig Latin. But he remembered the wry advice of one American ambassador to Egypt, concerning the study of Arabic, and had to smile. The ambassador told a student of the language that it would take years of diligent effort, and then he would finally have the key . . . to an empty room.

"Better just stick to English," Welles told the major. Then he hurried off to check facts about the landing for his broadcast.

This was July 17, 1958. All Westerners were warned to stay off the streets, for no one yet knew how the Jordanian Arabs would receive their British guests.

Welles is of the opinion that such orders never apply to newsmen, but this time he decided that they were tailor-made for newsmen's wives. So I had been grounded. Armed with books, stationery, and enough Jordanian dinars to keep the lemonade and coffee supply lines operative during my vigil, I camped at a round white iron table on the hotel terrace and tried to play tourist.

It was very pleasant at first. Clear hot sun beat down on the formal gardens facing me over the terrace rail. Beyond, excavated sandstone arches shaded portions of semicircular amphitheater benches where Roman citizens watched stage dramas in Jesus's day. There was no traffic along the road except for a bleating flock of sheep guided by its shepherd, who wore a long white robe and carried a crook. Then came a succession of Biblical travelers: old men astride white asses so small that the riders' feet dangled only an inch from the ground; then a trio of silent women gowned to the bare toe in black, seeming to float effortlessly over the pebbled road balancing meter-high earthen jugs on their heads. I felt suspended among the centuries.

Then a taxi hooted its way down the road, scattering sheep, shepherd, silent women and all, and suddenly I was back in the twentieth century again. The sights here had changed little with time, but the land was now called Jordan and it was on the brink of another war. While I was sitting here dreaming, my husband was out roaming the streets, perhaps stumbling into the opening shots of that war this very minute. I remembered stories out of Baghdad where mobs had killed three Americans who happened to be out in that city. Jordanians might follow the brutal lead of their Iraqi brothers and murder everyone in sight. No one knew what might happen, and when emotions run high anything is possible.

It seemed hours before Welles reappeared, and when he did I ran the full length of the terrace to meet him.

"Darling, are you all right?" I asked. "What's happening out there? Was there trouble?"

"It is quieter in the streets than it is right here," he said, looking at me curiously. "What's the matter with you, Pat? I've never seen you like this."

"I was worried about you. That's all," I said, leading him back to my white iron bivouac. "I'm glad you're back."

"Listen, baby," Welles said after we were seated and had ordered cold beers, "you never have to worry about me. You should know that by now. We have been out there together enough times for you to know I'm careful. I want to report the story standing up, not from a hospital bed. Now, please?"

I smiled and shook my head. "I know, dear. I really *do* know. But I seem to have this damned imagination to cope with sometimes. And I love you," I added, putting a hand on his arm, "and I just get scared."

I kissed him then and said, "So what *is* going on out there, my love? You *still* haven't told me."

Welles described the airport landings then and told me of his tours through town. Amman's streets were empty and quiet with only the plodding boots of policemen breaking the hot silence. Neither demonstrations nor riots disturbed the city dust. Citizens kept their counsel well within their homes, waiting for events to discover *them.* Even King Hussein remained tucked inside his limestone palace surrounded by prognosticating aides, while British troops camped at the airport, staying clear of town by about ten miles.

"And now that they are here," Welles concluded, "nobody knows what to do with them. The British themselves don't know what they are supposed to do, so the whole pack is just sitting at the airport sipping tea.

"In fact"—he chuckled—"the major problem of the day is whether the local food is safe for the boys. The whole command is pondering this one and they will probably be requesting volunteers soon for the hazardous duty of *eating.*"

Then he asked if I would like to go with him to the broadcasting studios when he finished his scripts. I was glad to be released from my prison of inaction, and from the sound of things I knew that my coin had flipped back to heads.

On the outskirts of Amman along the road to the airport there is a small rocky hill, or *jebel* in Arabic. It would have been indistinguishable from dozens of other brown wheatfield foothills surrounding the city except for a boxlike corrugated shed crouched on its crest. Aerials stretched high from the roof of the shed and over its single door was the sign: CABLE & WIRELESS. This was Amman's transmitting site. In the air around its tarpaper roof hovered electric signals relaying all cable and international telephone traffic for Jordan's capital. Not very impressive to the eye, but suitable for the ear since it was operated by a British commercial firm.

A few paces from the transmitter shack stood an old bus, well into retirement. It had no wheels, and its belly rested on an irregular bed of rocks. It must have been sleek and brightly painted once upon a time but now it had no color at all. Just rust, sun-baked rust. The weathered sign over its front visor announced with moribund pride that this bus was named "Liverpool," denoting either its ancestral home or a desire long frustrated by the layers of grit beneath its hood.

"There before you lies, or rather *lists*, Amman's broadcasting studio," Welles said as our taxi churned up the trackless hill and stopped beside Liverpool.

"Note the modern lines, the functional design," he continued. "To appreciate technological progress fully, you must step inside with me. But don't forget to duck. The door is so low that Liverpool must have been a kindergarten bus in its last life."

We climbed out of our car and were heading for the bus when Welles said, "Ah, here comes our faithful monitor now. Sometimes late, but never absent!"

Around Liverpool's sagging rear fender loped a huge tawny shepherd dog, barking happily at the sight of company. His outsized paws churned clouds of dust as he bounded to greet us and his thick furry tail drew joyous arcs in the air. He bathed our arms and legs lovingly before we scrambled up the bus steps and he even planted an affectionate "llaaap" on Welles' cheek, which we interpreted as best wishes for the broadcast.

We boarded Liverpool, laughing and trying to dry off some of that lavish welcome. Then I stopped dead. The bus was completely empty! All of the seats were gone except one lonely slat shelf in the rear. Steering wheel, driver's stool, gearshift, even most of the dash panel—all had been stripped away. Liverpool was a hollow shell seared with heat, and I found myself pitying the poor old bus as if it were a human derelict. Then with a shudder I began to pity Welles.

"But you can't broadcast from here," I said, appalled. "It is stifling. And there is no microphone or desk or . . ." But Welles had already walked through to the rear of the bus and was talking to a Jordanian technician. I watched in shocked silence as he perched stiffly on the lone remaining slat seat, pulled a small tippy table in front of him in the center of which rested a midget mike, and adjusted a set of damp, bent earphones on his head.

Then: "Hello, New York. Hello, New York! This is Amman, Jordan. Hello, hello. Come in please," Welles pleaded into the microphone, mopping his brow. At which point a dull regular thudding on the outside wall of the bus resounded through the silence.

"So sorry," said the distracted technician. "Whenever my dog hears a voice he likes, he leans against the bus to listen. That is his tail you hear wagging. He likes you, Mr. Hangen," he added, hoping to please. "You are lucky. When he doesn't like somebody's voice, he howls."

I knew my duty without being cued. That constant wag of approval would carry like a triphammer to New York's receivers, making the broadcast inaudible. I raced for the door before my husband's anguish could become more acute, jumped out of the bus, enveloped the big furry dog in my arms, and tugged him away.

At a safe distance, where his tail could connect only with air, I sat down beside him on the rocky ground. With one restraining arm around his giant ruff, I began to croon: "Hello, New York, hello," and concocted one of the most hair-raising broadcasts yet heard by man or dog. By the time Welles had finished his transmission, I was covered with the wettest kudos any correspondent ever received!

58

9

Every Inch a King

By this time the Philadelphia Hotel was bulging. Never before had there been such a paucity of rooms in scorching mid-July, but this year mad dogs, Englishmen, and Americans were knocking each other over trying to squeeze *into* the noonday sun. Amman was an inferno, but still the visitors came. All journalists, of course. And more British troops to swell the ranks of those already unemployed at the airport.

The staid old Philadelphia was converted overnight into a Press Club. Little old ladies with lace handkerchiefs who once nibbled biscuits in the lounge were replaced by obtrusive newsmen, tieless, with rolled shirtsleeves, typing bulletins frantically. Leisurely midmorning breakfasts were things of the past; now harried waiters ran the clock around trying to keep water jugs filled, coffee pots hot, icebuckets frozen, and the pantry stocked with mixers. Two days after the British press descended en masse, there was not a single bottle of tonic water to be found in all Amman. (Rumor has it that an R.A.F. Beverly met this crisis by jettisoning a load of paratroopers in favor of Schweppes, and although this cannot be verified, the drought *was* of short duration.) The hotel was a three-ring Piccadilly Circus. And I loved it.

I had never met Fleet Street up close before, but Amman in those days had representatives from most British newspapers as well as the BBC, and I found them charming, if a bit mad. American wire services, networks, and newspapers had men in town too, of course, and for the first time I saw the contrast in methods with which the two groups work. American correspondents, while protecting their beats with dog-bone ferocity, generally tip one another on routine news breaks. And they frequently work together, filling each other in on missing details. The more staid British papers and the BBC operate similarly, but the Penny Press tabloids of Britain are the profession's happy mavericks. They exhibit all the friendly cooperative instincts of subway commuters. Every man for himself and it is your turn to stand drinks for the house if you lose. No doubt on vacations they are good friends, but when a news story is hot they show tendencies that would drive Margaret Mead into science fiction.

One night the Fleet Streeters were assembled in the hotel lounge, eyeing each other suspiciously over throbbing typewriters. Suddenly one noticed that a colleague was missing. All work came to an immediate halt while a posse was formed to search for the miscreant who, it was naturally assumed, was out stealing a beat while their backs were turned. Tempers rose. The room was blue with righteous indignation. And nobody returned to his work until the culprit was dragged in, sleepy-eyed, yawning, in bathrobe and slippers. Even his churned bed sheets did not convince the rest that he had simply retired early. He was forced to nap in a lounge armchair until midnight when the cable office closed. After twelve, the vigil ended because no news could be cabled out until morning.

Elaborate ruses are often devised to escape this collective duenna, but they rarely work. That same night, the London Daily Mail informed one and all that he had filed his last story for the day. Selecting a paperback mystery, he retired quietly to a corner of the lounge to read. At a quarter to twelve, Daily Mail rose and headed slowly for the men's room. Fleet Street watched him go. No one intervened. Then, just as nonchalantly, the Express and the Telegraph got up from their chairs and went in the opposite direction out the front door. A few minutes later all three returned, together. Daily Mail had been nabbed in the rear of the hotel as he was climbing out the bathroom window on his way to the cable office. He had hoped to file a

60

last story just under the deadline and score a beat on the group. But all he got was a very red face, a barked shin, and a staggering new bar bill.

If something really big is afoot, however, British and Americans alike stop baring their teeth and get along like a team of Alaskan huskies. The morning when King Hussein unexpectedly called a press conference revealed this dormant spirit.

No one had been able to see the dapper young king since the British paratroop landing, and every journalist in town had been trying desperately to storm the palace gates. But of those at the hotel when the king's summons came, not one thought of keeping the news to himself. Instead each raced to the phones to spread the word through the press corps. Then we squeezed into taxis and hedgehopped up the winding private road to the king's palace.

"Wonder what the boy will tell us," mused the Daily Mail.

"Nothing serious, for sure," answered the Telegraph. "That kid hasn't had a responsible thought in his life."

"The way he cracks up sports cars is a real crime," chimed in the New York Times. "The minute he gets a new Thunderbird or Porsche, wham, he wrecks it."

"Or loses the ignition key and buys a whole new car," added the Tribune.

But when we reached Basman Palace, all levity ceased. The aura of the place was creepy, as if Iraq's murders had in fact taken place here. Its rambling low limestone walls were mottled with baleful shadows and the black-uniformed Circassian guards with their fuzzy black Astrakhan hats looked as though they had forgotten how to smile. The opulence of those silent rooms was in cloying contrast with their deep mourning. For the royalty of Jordan and Iraq are of the same Hashemite family, and now only the Jordanian branch remained. A night of murder in Baghdad had sounded its hollow death rattle over Amman. Hussein's palace echoed it.

We filed into a long reception room lighted by morning sun streaming in between corded velvet draperies at the windows. A narrow oak banquet table which would seat eighty comfortably made an island in the center of the room. We arranged ourselves in carved wooden armchairs along its sides, waiting for our host to take the crowned chair at the head. It was a long wait, made pleasant by scores of footmen who hovered behind our chairs offering long Virginia cigarettes embossed with golden crowns, and tiny white coffee cups etched in gold and royal blue. This was a new experience for me so I was happy for the delay, but my companions were champing at their cups.

The coffee was thick and perfumed. The taste was piquant, slightly heady, and too sweet for my liking, but I felt bound to finish it for the sake of politeness. Since the delicate cups had neither handles nor saucers, this was difficult to do.

Holding the hot little cup gingerly, I finished the coffee in a succession of quick sips and felt that I had done my duty as a guest. But I had not reckoned with those royal footmen dogging our backs like solicitous nannies. No sooner had I put my cup down than a black-sleeved arm stretched over my shoulder, the white-gloved hand clasping a long-spigotted brass ewer, ready to pour more coffee.

"No, thank you very much," I said, with a slight shake of my head.

The footman smiled, nodded, and filled my cup.

Obviously my rapport with royal footmen left something to be desired.

Again I drank the coffee, at great cost to my smarting fingers. One *must* be well mannered in palaces.

The black arm and white hand started their forward stretch again. In the nick of time I put two fingers across the mouth of my cup, smiled up at the footman and said, clearly, "No thank you. No more coffee, thank you."

He returned my smile, withdrew his arm and stood quietly at my side. Good for me! My lessons in one-upmanship were paying off.

But the moment my fingers left the cup it was filled again, with a sleight of hand I would not have believed possible. I almost whimpered. Manners decreed that I empty my cup, but short of grabbing the footman's arm on the next go-round, I could not imagine a way to shut off this gushing spigot.

Then I noticed that nobody else seemed to be having this problem. Their cups stood empty, cool, untouched. It seemed that I was the only one under attack. Why?

"Honey," I whispered to Welles who was seated beside me studying his notes, "this coffee is making me dizzy. Please tell the man to stop before I float away!"

"If you don't want any more," he replied with a laugh, "you must rock your cup back and forth like this," and he began tipping his little cup slowly from side to side on the table. "If you don't, they'll keep it filled forever."

He was right. I rocked my cup once or twice and, lo, my tormentor left me alone. By that time, however, it would not have mattered anyway because the room suddenly became hushed. The king was entering.

We stood. Hussein's bearing as he strode the length of that room to his chair was that of a man "every inch a king." His eyes were red from weeping, but his shoulders were determinedly straight. His lips were thin and pale in a face boyish a few days before, but now grimly aged, its pallor accentuated by the bristly black of his mustache and thick black hair. This was not a weak man. Frivolous perhaps he had been, capricious and selfish. But no longer. His manner this day conveyed mature strength.

We followed his lead in seating ourselves, and waited.

There was no sound in the room. The king sat straight, his hands gripping the arms of his chair. He wore a dark-blue Western suit and black tie, but no crown. There was a sense of humility about him that seemed to suggest that he had left off his crown for a reason. Before, he had treated that insignia as a plaything, but the murders in Iraq now gave it solemn meaning: Hashemite crowns could either evoke responsible strength or be smashed in the dust under the feet of frenzied mobs. Could Hussein accept so heavy a role? We sat silently, waiting to hear.

Then he began to speak.

"It is with a heavy and distressed heart that I must inform you that news is now available."

The king spoke so softly that we swayed toward him, straining to hear. He did not look at us. His eyes were fixed on the table before him.

In a tremulous voice, he continued: "Murderers and rebels from the United Arab Republic assassinated my 'brother' Feisal with the crown prince and all members of the royal family. These are only the latest in a long caravan of martyrs whom our family has given for the good of the Arab world. And they are not the last. They died working to defend the Arab world and Arab nationalism. We are ready to do the same."

Hussein looked up, straightened, and met our eyes in turn.

"But we will continue to work to serve our people," he said in a stronger voice. "We will see that the blood which was shed was not shed in vain."

Then, with sudden force, the king said, "Our first objective is to save ourselves from falling prey to international Communism which is moving through Egypt and Syria to destroy the independence and freedom of this kingdom. They shall not prevail!"

I wanted to cheer. This twenty-three-year-old boy had suddenly become a man. There was no vibrato in his voice now. It was level and confident. Whether or not his thesis was right, no one could fail to admire him.

But if I had cheered I would have been disowned by my colleagues, and very possibly divorced. So I remained quiet until the end.

"We have the unquestioned loyalty of the army and the people," Hussein continued. "Iraq has fallen victim of plots. We shall restore order and peace to Iraq. We have asked help from our friends whose prompt response has added to our self-confidence. The banner of freedom shall be kept flying high in the free world!"

That was it. The question period brought little else. Clearly Hussein did not know what methods could be used to achieve his aims. The British breakwater was intact. He wanted American troops to move in as well, and ultimately settled for an airlift of fuel supplies. But no one could have predicted that in the days to follow, Jordan would neither panic into violence nor capitulate.

64

There was little discussion in our crowded taxi as we rattled back down that royal hill. The sarcasm of our uphill drive was gone. Everyone liked the boy king now and admired his show of strength, but who in honesty could have conceded him the slightest chance of success? Whoever could was not among us that day.

But as we have seen since, our pessimism proved empty. Hussein has become one of the strongest leaders in the Middle East, and Jordan *has* lived on.

Welles and I returned to our third-floor oven feeling extremely subdued. An experience of that sort is exhausting, intellectually and emotionally, and results in a curious physical depletion. But this was no time for relaxing: there was a broadcast to be made. While Welles warmed up the typewriter, I went over my notes in case he needed them, and we spent the next half hour discussing all that we had heard. Then Welles wrote his scripts and we were off for the bus named Liverpool.

When we returned, we had a late lunch and then decided to give in to the drowsing combination of heat and emotional exhaustion.

The temperature hovered at about 110 degrees. We stretched out beside our rattling green fan and succumbed to inertia. But just before we dropped off to sleep, I was dimly conscious of dull plop-plop-plop sounds coming from the yard below our windows.

"What on earth?" I mumbled sleepily and got up to investigate, certain that the noises could not be human-inspired, for no one would break the siesta tradition in such heat as this. Or if they did, it would have to be for the most compelling of reasons.

I looked out of the window, then shook my head in disbelief.

There, on the tennis courts bordering the hotel, were Daily Express and Daily Mail facing each other perspiringly across the net. Their serves were apathetic and they staggered for their returns, but each preferred to die of heat stroke rather than to allow the other out of his sight.

"What a crazy profession," I murmured, crawling back on the bed. "You don't have to be mad, but it helps."

65

10

Get Thee Unto Pharaoh

Terrorist bombs were exploding all over Amman those days. One blew apart the American economic aid office and another fell just short of gutting the British Council library. Syrians were infiltrating into Jordan by droves. Caches of illegal arms were discovered daily. Egypt's President Nasser issued denunciations of King Hussein, and Cairo Radio called for his assassination. The Egyptian Embassy burned its papers and was expelled from Jordan. Black mourning flags flew from taxi fenders and atop government buildings in memory of Iraq's murders. Strike petitions circulated protesting the presence of British troops, and the rumble of corrugated blinds as they were pulled down over shop fronts echoed throughout the city.

But the nights were completely quiet, so in that sense it was a correspondent's dream. Or at least his wife's. The hours during the day when Welles was working were more than made up for during our evenings together. We frequently left the Philadelphia for the slight variety of having dinner at the Amman Club which boasted a modern bar and jazz combo. And when we walked there and back, the streets were totally deserted. It was as if the sun in setting was playing Pied Piper and taking all residents with it. With the exception of one or two policemen, whose shadows loomed like silent sentries in the moonlit streets, we never met a soul. The hot night air was heavy with the scent of jasmine but not even a breeze disturbed the stillness.

One evening when we returned to the Philadelphia after

strolling through the blackened town, the heat was still so oppressive we decided to have a nightcap on the patio before braving our steaming room. The garden seemed deserted when we entered, but from a corner table came a wave of invitation. It was Richard Hunt, the personable and talented *New York Times* correspondent who has since joined NBC. Dick had stationed himself directly beneath a huge fan and the air rippled through his short blond hair like wind through wheat.

"Too damn hot to sleep," Dick said, heaping more ice into his gin and tonic. "I hear you've got an air-conditioner. You are lucky."

Welles and I exchanged glances and grinned.

"Sure," Welles retorted, "it is green and it rattles. Has about as much churning power as a dying butterfly."

"If we do manage to get to sleep, its groaning wakes us up again," I added. "However, it's company."

Dick looked sympathetic. "In that case," he said, motioning to the waiter, "two more gins and tonic, fast!"

"Pat and I are thinking of leaving soon," Welles told Dick, as my mouth dropped open in amazement.

"Pat has been thinking of leaving for a long time," I said to nobody in particular since nobody was listening, "but this is the first she's heard that there might be a chance."

"Seems pretty quiet," continued Welles, ignoring my interruption. "My guess is that these petty snipings and bombings will drag on and nothing will really happen until Hammarskjöld arrives. How does it look to you?"

Dick shrugged and crunched an ice cube slowly.

"Agreed," he said. "I'm trying to get out too, but the *Times* apparently wants me to hang on." Then he laughed, adding, "Poor old Rawle isn't having much luck with his cable battle, by the way."

Welles chuckled at this, but I was mystified. "You mean Rawle Knox of the London *Observer?*" I asked. "What is he up to? And isn't he sitting over there, by the way?" I pointed across the patio to a lone husky figure, sitting at a table well stocked with bar supplies, thumbing wildly through a book. "Good heavens," I added, looking more closely. "It looks like he is studying the Bible."

Welles laughed. "He is. That's the beauty of it. Rawle's been firing off cables to the *Observer* trying to get transferred out of here. He is taking his cable texts from the Bible, figuring that is the best way around censorship in the Holy Land."

"The first one was great," chimed in Dick, and told us how Rawle had dusted off his hotel room Gideon the night before, sat down at his typewriter and composed the following cable:

THE OBSERVER, LONDON
EX. 4:18 (signed) KNOX

It is to be assumed that Rawle's editor at the other end of the line is a religious man himself. He consulted his Bible and deciphered the message as reading: "Let me go, I pray thee, and return unto my brethren which are in Egypt, and see whether they be yet alive."

The reply had bounced back a few hours ago:

KNOX, PHILADELPHIA HOTEL, AMMAN
HE. 13:17 (signed) OBSERVER

The verse cited read: "Obey them that have the rule over you, and submit yourselves; for they watch for your souls, as they that must give account, that they may do it with joy, and not with grief: for that *is* unprofitable for you."

Bloody but unbowed, Rawle had brought his Gideon to the patio with him this evening. I couldn't wait to hear his reply, and looked over at his table just in time to see him get up with a jubilant expression on his face. He closed his Gideon with a slam, picked up his drink, and headed our way. Rawle is a stocky man but light on his feet, and this night he all but floated between his table and ours.

"Think I've found it at last!" crowed Rawle. "How does this sound? 'Observer London, dash, John 16:7, dash, Knox'?"

"Sounds staccato to me," said Welles. "What does it mean?"

"No student of the Bible, eh?" taunted Rawle; but I wasn't impressed, having watched him laboriously ploughing through that Good Book for the past hour.

"It means," Rawle continued, " 'Nevertheless I tell you the truth; it is expedient for you that I go away: for if I go not away, the Comforter will not come unto you; but if I depart I will send him unto you.' "

"Great!" Dick exclaimed. "You mean that you have some hot stories that you can't file from here because of censorship, and will cable from somewhere outside? Boy, that ought to do it as nothing else could."

Welles nodded, adding, "Right. I've yet to know an editor who would pass that up. Have you got them?"

"I'll *get* them," said Rawle and wandered dazedly off to bed.

"If I thought that the *Times* had a Bible I might try it," Dick said. "Sure wish something would happen."

Dick Hunt is wasting his time in journalism. He could be the world's greatest seer, for he had no sooner spoken those wishful words than three shots shattered the silence.

Both men were on their feet in a second. Welles murmured, "They're close." Dick nodded. "Right in front of the hotel, sounds like," he said. And the next thing I knew, I was sitting alone in the patio, watching Welles and Dick disappearing at a gallop around the side of the hotel.

Here we go again, I thought, taking a long sip of my drink. Why do I put up with this madness? There must be another way to love a man. The glamorous life I had dreamed of was deteriorating into a game of chance, and at that moment I wasn't sure that I liked it.

But just then, around the garden walk came Welles and Dick, springing along with light steps, hooting with laughter.

"These people!" exclaimed Welles. "What can you *do* with people like this?"

"Love 'em and leave 'em," chortled Dick. "I give up!"

"Well, *tell* me," I said, feeling exasperated with them both. "It didn't sound funny at all from here. What happened?"

"Nothing at all," Welles answered. "Just one of those trigger-happy guards in front of the hotel. Thought he heard something in the dark, so he started shooting."

"The only trouble was," Dick cut in, "his aim was a bit bad. He fired like crazy . . . and shot his own foot. One bullet in the foot and two in the ground. And these are the fellows who are supposed to protect us!"

"That does it," said Welles suddenly. "Let's go pack and head for Beirut in the morning. At least the Lebanese don't shoot *themselves*. This part of the world has enough holy feet without making more."

"Your pun is awful," I said, "but your idea is great. It will be good to get back to Beirut."

"Good night, Dick," Welles said, clapping his friend on the back. "I'll leave my Bible at the desk for you." And we left to pack.

After Welles's broadcast the next morning, we checked out of the hotel, preparing to leave for Jerusalem. We were stowing our baggage in the trunk of the car when Rawle Knox bounded out on the hotel porch with his baggage.

"Rawle!" I called. "Are you leaving? What happened?"

He handed me the cable he had received from London. "It came late last night," he said, beaming like a neon sign.

Unfolding it, I read:

KNOX, PHILADELPHIA HOTEL, AMMAN
EX. 7:15 (signed) OBSERVER

"It says," he explained, " 'Get thee unto Pharaoh in the morning.' So I have made a plane reservation to Cairo and am leaving with a prayer of thanksgiving."

We all said goodbye, knowing we would meet soon in Egypt, and Welles and I climbed into our car. Finally we could have our communion with the silver olive trees, although it would have to be only an overnight stand since duty called in Beirut the following day.

About an hour down the Jerusalem road from Amman is a right turnoff which dives into an endless ochre valley sided by porous lavender mountains. It is the lavender of shade, constantly moving shade which meanders among jagged crevices

70

but never visits the valley floor. South in this valley, hidden among orchard gardens, entwined by ageless climber vines, is an ancient Roman city: Jerash. Jerash, the proud columned city of the Antonines. The creature of moneychangers, of legionnaires. Now in ruins but still living.

Anxious though we were to return to Jerusalem, we could not resist taking that right turn to discover for ourselves how Jerash lives. And weird and wonderful it is. Profuse life unsullied by the Coke bottle and postcard.

We parked in a grove of tangled scrub oak and took the narrow footpath indicated to us by our driver. The sun was hot. There was no sound save the buzzing of bees and an occasional bird song. We were alone, walking up the silent teeter-totter of time; within moments our board would flip its angle of slope and deposit us in a world twenty centuries old.

We came to the end of our path. There ahead was Rome, the extract of her ancient glory, distilled by time. A high sculpted limestone gateway opened on the triumphal way, floored with wasting stone blocks, tapered by centuries of footsteps. Clumps of tiny lavender and white perennials gave a nap to the way. Other blossoms poked sturdy fingers through stone walls that were once shops: dead stones that had long since conceded supremacy to living plants.

Off to one side of the triumphal way loomed an amphitheater, well-preserved, haughty. Shaggy snickering goats were tethered in the orchestra. To the other side, a sun temple: desolate, broken, a jumble of finely hewn stones. Barefoot children clambered over sculptured noseless heroes.

And coming to meet us along the triumphal way were random groups of the Empire's inheritors, Circassians who built their village adjoining the ancient city with stones extracted from its walls. First, a brown child, unclothed except for a faded blue cloth shirt, trailing a stick, listening to it tick off the ancient road stones. Then an ageless woman, slim, lithe, balancing a pottery jug on her head: Her black-gowned figure seemed to float because she touched only the ball of her foot to the stones; her trunk swayed but her shoulders could be cast in bronze. She

71

is expressionless and makes no sound. She wafts by us like a breeze. Later, a flock of jingle-bell goats, sometimes led, sometimes followed by its boy shepherd. Old men with sun-parched skins and gray hair riding sideways on donkeys which clop-clop across right-angled intersections to our road: crinkled skin, cracked rock. And young men riding their beasts astride.

The worn stone streets of Jerash, laid out in geometric precision, bear a pulsing stream of life. Today's children in yesterday's sand castles. Stones which once endured the stamp of Roman boots now are polished by bare brown feet and cloven hoofs. It is a deeply impressive sight because neither these people nor their ancestors felt constrained to level the old to make way for the new. Instead they live among these noble columns with the same equanimity with which they prune the fruit trees that intersperse the stone and provide their livelihood.

In Jerash the meek have inherited both the earth and these products of man's genius which grace it, and with a refreshing lack of contrivance they combine the two in the composure of everyday life. Change, and no change. Flux set in constancy. We left with renewed awareness of the boundlessness of life, and our contemplative mood accompanied us as we wound up out of the Jerash valley and swung onto the main road southwest to Jerusalem. Nothing we saw along the mudcaked edges of the Dead Sea or among the sunburned rocky hills of Judea lessened it. But when we rounded the last turn in the precipitous chain of hills rising out of the Dead Sea flat to drop into the bowl of Jerusalem, our contemplation ended, only to begin again in a major key. For there, rising from the crest of the hill facing us across an easy divide, were the crenelated city walls.

We went first to the Old City, that portion of Arab Jerusalem within the ancient walls. We followed the Way of the Cross, up gnarled cobbled streets, past artisan stalls where crafts have lived by filiation for centuries, around blunt turnings where we searched out dim signs marking succeeding Stations, to the Holy Sepulchre.

It is hard to hold the vision fast when your sleeves are tugged every inch of the way. Within that awesome edifice, awe fights for survival while creatures of a score of faiths entreat you to visit their dim stalls with assurance that theirs is the *true* resting place of Christ. After a dozen such conflicting pledges, one feels impelled to clasp belief firmly to breast and preserve it by fleeing. Left alone again, the spirit soars.

We wandered on, breathing, observing, loving. Forever stopping one another by a touch of the hand or a word, sharing impressions that demand sharing. At the Wailing Wall we spoke not at all.

Leaving the Old City, we passed by the Mandelbaum Gate. The one-way gate. The strait gate through which one may enter Israel without return. An unimpressive gate, unless one reads between the rocks. Literally a hole in the wall.

And Welles and I shared something else. Tucked away among palm trees and wildflowers in a cleft in a hill called Calvary is a small unassuming cavern hollowed from the rock. There is an upright slab of stone resting against one side, a slab that could have been rolled away from the opening. And could have exposed an empty tomb. We spent more than an hour resting there and sharing the fulfillment of our individual quests for meaning, which, unbidden, had proved the same.

The Garden Tomb joined that highly select company of images which shall always live just behind my mind's eye.

We could have invested weeks and months in that Scriptural land, but flying off to Beirut the next morning, we both felt that we had experienced enough for one visit. We knew that upon our return to Jerusalem another day we would build on those impressions and make them part of ourselves.

We were right. This has happened. Curious that it should, however, for we have never been back.

11

Leave Canceled

"What have you got against that poor croissant?" Welles asked across the breakfast table one morning about a month after our return to Beirut. We were sitting on the sunny balcony off our hotel room and I was playing listlessly with my roll, deep in thought.

Welles pointed to the pile of crumbs beside my plate and said, "Looks like you're planning to feed birds."

I hadn't been aware of the mess I was making. I swept the flakes off onto a plate and said, "I'm just not very hungry this morning."

The truth was that a gloom-cloud the size of the Hindenburg was hovering over me. This whole business of revolution and hotel living had suddenly got to me. The situation in Lebanon had become ambiguous and tiresome, and I was sick to death of room-service meals. I would have given anything to go into my own kitchen and just make a cup of coffee for a change.

Welles was watching me thoughtfully. Then he got up from the table and went into the room to make a phone call. He was smiling broadly when he returned.

"How would you like to go out to a nightclub tonight?" he asked. "I think we've been at this thing too hard. We need a little relaxation. Okay with you?"

Some joke, I thought resentfully. Very funny man, my husband. Here we are in a city that is completely shut down by an all-night curfew. There had been no night life at all for three whole months.

"Please, honey," I said, "I feel low enough this morning without that. Sure I'd like to go nightclubbing. I'd also like to fly to Rome for the weekend, or have a gimlet lunch at Sardi's."

"But I mean it," Welles said. "I heard a rumor that the Black Cat has been operating illegally as a curfew club. Locked doors, pulled shades, speakeasy stuff. I've just checked and it's all true. So I've made reservations for tonight. Dinner, dancing, the works. How about it?"

"Oh Welles, I'd love it," I said, brightening. "I feel better already." I decided right then to spend the whole day doing wonderfully ordinary things like polishing nails and having my hair done. Maybe even buy a new dress. No bullets, no bombs. Just carefree, happy expectation.

As it turned out, I could have spent those hours far more profitably stuffing kapok into sleeping bags. For that evening ended with all the gaiety of a vagrancy lockup.

The Black Cat was fine. Soft lights, music, food: all excellent and just exactly what we needed. We had a wonderful time, dancing every dance and enjoying every bite. But when we decided we'd had enough and wanted to go home to bed, we found that we couldn't get out.

"But look," Welles argued with the manager at two o'clock in the morning, "we're tired and I want my wife to get some rest. Won't you please unlock the door and let us go?"

"Sorry, sir," our host said with a yawn, "I can't open the door until five o'clock and I'm tired too. It's this ridiculous curfew."

"But look," I said, like a sleepy parrot, "we have curfew passes. It's all right for us to be on the street at *any* hour."

The manager shook his head. "It's not all right for you to be seen leaving my place at *this* hour," he explained. "For me, it would be finish. You do understand?" he urged. "Come, have a drink on the house."

That was exactly what we didn't want. Then from the far corner of the bar came something else we didn't want: "Down by the Old Mill Stream" being sung in aged-in-the-wood scotch harmony.

"Feel like singing?" Welles asked as we turned back toward our table.

"I feel like sleeping." I yawned. "I'll be a wreck if we don't.

There's that Marine visit tomorrow, remember? Do you suppose we could curl up over there in the corner?"

"It looks more comfortable than an airport lounge," Welles said, leading the way to a soft banquette, "and I've slept in a lot of those." He blew out the candles on adjoining tables, sat down, and motioned for me to stretch out with my head on his lap.

"You do make a nice pillow," I said, snuggling down to sleep.

"But are you comfortable like this?"

"I could sleep standing up, at this point," he answered. "Good night, honey. See you after curfew."

I must have slept soundly in spite of barbershop quartets, for it seemed I had just dropped off when Welles said, "Time to wake up. The padlock's off and I'm going to take you home."

Nightclubs in the morning are not attractive. Neither are satin dresses that have been slept in. I was eager to leave, yet I hated to be out on the streets looking like yesterday's parfait. I hoped for an insomniac taxi driver, and was relieved when we found a whole line of cabs waiting outside. Clearly the Black Cat's hours weren't such a secret after all. And we vowed that the next time we came, we would take naps in the afternoon and be prepared.

But this day presented a problem, and I hoped that I was rested enough to handle it. The ladies of Beirut's tiny Congregational Church had baked cakes and cookies for the U.S. Marines camped in the hills above town, and a delegation was taking them up by helicopter at nine o'clock this morning. Yesterday, when I felt more spritely, I had decided to try to accompany the flight. Welles thought it such a good idea that he had already planned a broadcast about it, so there was no backing out now.

"Good human interest," he had said. "Show how the Marines are living over here, quotes, color, all that. Why not take a cameraman along too and get something for television?"

So it was all set, and although I would have given anything to spend the day in bed, an NBC cameraman and I were in a taxi two hours later searching for a Marine helicopter loaded with cake. We found it perched on top of a rocky hill beside the sea, all ready to take off. It took some fast talking to get ourselves on board. The pilot was cooperative and the ladies were delighted to have their project televised, but the co-pilot muttered gloomily about weight and overcrowding.

"You can get aboard," he said, "and then we'll see if we can get off the ground. If not, we'll have to leave you behind." That sounded reasonable enough, just so he didn't try too hard and drop us right into the sea.

The engine began to roar as we fastened our straps. The noise was so great we couldn't even talk. Then the plane shook and bumped and slowly took off. It was like being inside an angry lion who had hiccups. We hovered so low over St. George's Bay that the plane got wet, but we soon turned inland to hedgehop over the crags and scrub of Lebanon's coastal foothills. At last we skimmed a ridge and dropped neatly onto a small saucer-shaped meadow. The engine roar stopped abruptly. We unbelted ourselves and jumped to the ground as a jeep-load of grinning, waving Marines appeared over the saucer's rim.

As the men loaded all of us into the jeep with our cakes and cookies, it became clear that their welcome had little to do with the traveling bakery. They were so glad to see new faces that we could have had two heads apiece and been met with equal warmth. The proud United States Marines were just plain bored.

"This is one hell of a war," grumbled the private on my left from under his stack of cake boxes. "We sit here in these rocks all day long and nothing ever happens."

"Old men used to hike up to sell us souvenirs when we first came," put in another, "but now the sentries won't let them in, so we don't see anybody. Great life!"

I suggested that just by being there they were doing a lot to restrain the Lebanese, and that they should be pleased that their presence had such a calming influence.

"Guess so," responded the private. "But our company hasn't been home in a long time. I can think of better places than this to sit around doing nothing."

The mess cook cut the cakes into Marine-sized shares soon after we arrived in camp, and troops queued in a serpentine along the hillside.

Suddenly an outraged howl broke from a tent close by.

"Snoopy!" shouted the voice. "You come back here, you no good hound-dog!" Out of the tent shot a little black-and-white mongrel, running for all he was worth, with a red-faced Marine in hot pursuit. The pup's nose was covered with sticky chocolate. A wedge of black cake crumbled from his mouth, and his tail was wagging like sixty.

"Hey, Pete, don't kill him!" called one of the boys near me. "I'm out of cigarettes already!" And others took up the cry, laughing and hooting.

The whole thing went over my head, until one of my guides explained that Snoopy was the company mascot and Pete his self-appointed guardian.

"Snoopy likes cigarettes?" I asked.

"Nope," corrected my guide. "We *bought* him for cigarettes. One package, American. From a Lebanese truck driver. Mistake, I guess."

"Bad dog?" I asked.

"Nope," he said, shaking his head. "Good dog. Nothing wrong with Snoopy. But word got around the mountains and for the next full week every Lebanese within miles brought us scrawny animals, hoping we'd buy. Canteen almost ran out of cigarettes before the captain ordered people kept away from camp." Then he grinned and said, "Want to see George?"

George turned out to be a moth-eaten little donkey, but he was a rare treasure because he had cost real money: five whole dollars. Consequently he commanded as much respect as the company commander in this boresome bivouac.

The company fielded continuous patrols in the area but no rebel movements were reported. I wasn't surprised. If the revolution had proved nothing else, it had shown that Lebanon's rebels operate with clinical intent. They would never deliberately provoke a company of trained Marines. But even knowing this, I could hardly believe a formal report the captain showed me that had just come in from a perimeter outpost.

"Observed today: one old shepherd and a flock of sheep," it read. "Sheep looked hostile."

"Real report?" I asked, hoping life wasn't quite this dreary.

"Typical," replied the captain.

"Then please do me a favor," I said quickly. "Post a notice on the bulletin board. The first men who get leave from this hill are invited to our hotel in Beirut. There's a swimming pool, cold beer, and lots of odd characters in bikinis. The men will be our guests as long as they like. If we can't cook up something more exciting than angry sheep, we'd better quit."

Four days later, bright and early in the morning, there was a polite but firm knock on our hotel room door. Welles left the breakfast table and went in from our terrace to see who it was. I heard several voices, indistinct, questioning. Then Welles returned.

"Friends of yours," he said, a bit huffily I thought. "In fact, it looks like the whole damn Marine Corps."

"Oh gosh, I forgot," I said. "Meant to tell you. I'm sorry. They were so darn bored on that hillside, I just had to invite them." And I hurried to greet my guests. But not quickly enough to miss the scowl on my husband's face. He was actually jealous!

A few minutes later I returned to the terrace, feeling like the cat who swallowed the canary. The Marines had gone down to the swimming pool, but before they left, they said something very interesting.

"Poor dears," I said, deciding to have a little fun with Welles. "It's their first leave in months but they can only stay in town one night."

"Hmmmmm," he murmured, pretending to ignore me in his newspaper.

"They have to be back in camp tomorrow to pack up," I continued, trying to keep a straight face. "Their company is leaving Tuesday. It's a shame. Their first leave, and now this."

With that, Welles slowly lowered his paper, sat back, and studied me carefully.

"All right, baby, out with it," he said quietly. "*Where* are they going Tuesday?"

"Sailing," I said. "Their company is sailing back to the States. The Marines are being withdrawn from Lebanon, honey." I grinned. "We have ourselves a story!"

"You mean that?" he asked, springing from his chair. I nodded and we both started to laugh. He picked me up, swung me around, and said, "You scored a beat on all of us this time. And you know what? Anytime you want to invite friends home, it's all right with me."

Then he grabbed his notebook and pencil and headed for the door.

"Which way did they go?"

12

Persona Non Grata

Beirut had been our base for almost five months when a cable came, for me. It was my first in all the stacks of Hangen cables that had arrived during our Lebanese odyssey, so I opened it with some excitement.

"UNICEF wants me to go to Libya for them," I said to Welles, who was deep in his own pile of messages. "To do some stories on their children's aid projects."

"Sounds like fun," he replied, laying his papers aside. "Let's see it."

Welles studied the cable. "Benghazi, Tripoli, ten days, all expenses. You'll be in good hands too, sponsored by the United Nations. Sounds good." He smiled and then added: "And dear, while you are there, would you check around please to see how much influence Nasser has with the Libyans? I hear that they consider him the greatest thing to hit the Middle East since Cleopatra. They would rather go along with him and his Arab nationalism than with their own crown prince. There might even be a merger between Libya and Egypt soon." He handed the paper back, smiled brightly and kissed me.

"But I'm not sure I want to . . ." I started, feeling that the train was leaving the station a bit ahead of schedule.

"Could be a good story for NBC too," he concluded. "I'm glad that you're going."

That did it. Five months married and he was glad to be getting rid of me. Practically pushing me out! Laughing all the way.

"Well I'm not going," I said flatly. "Whether you care or not, I don't want to leave you. And I certainly don't like practically being thrown out of the door. If you want a story from Libya, *you* go get it!" And I started to leave the room.

Welles caught me at the door and spun me around.

"I didn't mean it that way and you know it," he said, looking straight into my eyes. "It is a fine assignment and something you could do very well. I'm proud of you, and I think that you should be damn pleased that UNICEF wants you.

"I don't want us to be apart either," he continued, more softly now, "but that's the way this business goes sometimes. I have to be back in Amman for Dag Hammarskjöld's visit, and then on to Baghdad for a day or two, now that it's open. If you would like to come along, fine. But I think that you might be happier doing the Libya thing for a change." He kissed me and added, "But of course it is up to you."

Then we were in each other's arms, my doubts were gone, my heart was full. And I went to Libya in the morning.

When I boarded that plane for Benghazi, however, it was still with some misgivings. I wished that we were going together. But better a fresh look at Libya than a rerun through the grit of Jordan. And my sadness at leaving Welles was eased by the knowledge that we would meet in Cairo in ten days and be together again. Back home in our own apartment which we had not seen since our wedding. Our first real home. I couldn't wait!

But in our happy planning we had not reckoned with the Egyptians.

Welles was in Baghdad when the word reached him that he had been declared persona non grata by the Egyptian government and would not be allowed to return to Cairo. I was winding up a fascinating ten days in Libya learning that UNICEF's food programs were impressively effective, and that Egypt's Nasser was indeed number-one Libyan hero, when Welles cabled me the news.

It was the night before I was to leave Benghazi. My UNICEF notes were strewn around the desk in my hotel room as I typed up final drafts of the news stories and background reports I had promised. Then came a knock at the door.

Grumbling at interruptions that shatter trains of thought, I went to open it for the smiling Libyan bellboy who offered me a cable. As I read it, the derailment was complete:

> I AM DECLARED PERSONA NON GRATA BY
> EGYPTIAN AUTHORITIES. FORBIDDEN RETURN
> CAIRO. NO REASON GIVEN. PLAN TRY TO
> RETURN BUT IF UNSUCCESSFUL WILL GO TO
> BEIRUT. ADVISE YOU RETURN CAIRO AS
> PLANNED. BELIEVE DECISION REVERSIBLE
> BUT ANYWAY WE HAVE EACH OTHER WHICH IS
> ALL THAT COUNTS. ALL LOVE. WELLES.

I sank into a chair and stared at nothing. What did this mean? What were they *doing* to him? Should I go to Cairo, or straight to Beirut where he probably was? No, he says to return to Cairo. Maybe he will get back there before I do after all. He says that it might be reversed. It probably will be. I had better go on to Cairo. But . . .

Then I noticed a last line on the cable. A note from the Benghazi cable office saying: "Correction to follow in text."

I stayed up all that long night waiting, praying that the decision had been reversed. But the correction never came.

That was one of the longest flights I have ever made. Our little DC-3 was so slow it seemed to flap its wings. The hours between Benghazi and Cairo crawled by. The trouble was that I did not know what to expect when I arrived. My experience in the Middle East was so limited at that point that I could not imagine what the Egyptian authorities would do. But I guess that I was lucky; those with broader knowledge would have flown the other way.

So on I flapped, wondering what would happen to Welles if he did not make it back. Or if he did, for that matter. And wondering, too, if they would even let *me* in.

I discovered a strange thing about fear that day, as our plane flew low over unbroken miles of North African desert sand. It is impossible to sustain. With time, fear mercifully erodes and anger begins filling the void. Time is the essential element, and I had so much of it that by the time we circled to land in Cairo, I was furious. My primary target was President Nasser himself for permitting his men to label my husband "Undesirable." Welles of all people! I almost laughed. How very little they knew. Well, Mr. President, I shall stage a hunger strike right on your front lawn until you invite Welles back again. We shall see what the world's press makes of *that*. And a pox on your pyramids too!

But I lost a lot of that healthy starch when the plane landed and I trudged toward customs with my co-passengers. Crowded behind the chicken wire that held them cleanly apart from us, the suspect, were Cairo residents on hand to greet arrivals. Search though I did through that mass of faces, I could not find Welles anywhere. So it had indeed happened: he had not been allowed back into Egypt, and I was completely alone.

It was a real blow. But then I took a deep breath and decided there was only one thing to do: proceed. So, taking my place in the customs line, I slowly approached the famous Blue Book.

Most Middle Eastern countries have thick looseleaf binders listing names of people whom they consider unacceptable and who are sent right back out on any departing airplane. Maybe all countries have similar books, but Egypt is the only one I know of that keeps it right on top of the counter. It loomed as large that day as *Who's Who* and looked twice as formidable.

The couple in front of me passed muster, and then it was my turn. The inspector flipped the book open to H, his finger starting down the column and suddenly stopping. He read, frowned, looked up at me, and read again. I almost bolted. *Any* flight out would be better than an Egyptian jail. But just as I was figuring my chances of escaping, the officer suddenly nodded, smiled, and motioned me on. I had cleared! Back in Cairo, safe and sound. Yes, but for what?

This was a new low but fortunately short lived, because at that moment John and Jeanne Hogan, our dear friends from the American Embassy, pushed through the crowd, wrapped me in warm hugs, and led me to their car for the drive into town.

"John," I asked as we climbed into the car, "what *is* this all about; do you know? What has happened?"

"Sweetie, we just don't know," he answered, slipping his arm around me. "The whole thing hit the embassy like a bombshell. We've dropped everything, trying to find out. But so far," he said and he shook his head, "we haven't got a thing. Welles is out, but nobody can find out *why.*"

"Where is he now?" I continued quietly, suddenly feeling very tired. "Did he make it to Beirut, do you know?"

"Yes, he is there," John answered. "Bill Landrey talked to him by phone today. He is worried but okay, and he plans to fight it of course. Bill wants to see you as soon as you can make it."

"Oh good!" I was relieved that *someone* had made contact. "Let's go now, please, can we? I must know what they talked about."

So off we went to see Wilbur G. Landrey, the first-rate newsman then heading the United Press International bureau in Cairo. Bill had been a member of our wedding party here five months ago, but although he was one of Welles' closest friends, I hadn't had the chance to know him well until now.

He was working on a story when I arrived at his UPI office, and he seemed surprised and relieved to see me.

"Pat!" he exclaimed, jumping up from his desk. "You made it. Did you have any trouble getting in? Welles was more worried about you than about himself when I talked to him." Then he frowned and added gently, "I only wish that we could let him know."

"Why don't we phone him, Bill," I said excitedly. "I want so much to talk to him and hear how he is."

"We can't," Bill countered. "I got through this morning by pure luck. Some censor hadn't had the word. But now"—he shrugged—"the tap on my phone sounds like a triphammer. I guess they are pretty angry, but God only knows why."

Samia Megalli, Bill's attractive assistant, came in with coffee at that moment and I could have hugged her. My knees had weakened abruptly with Bill's words and I sank into a chair and

85

sipped the strong Turkish brew gratefully. Then I noticed that they both were watching me closely, with some concern.

"Look"—I smiled—"I'm all right. Just a little tired and very worried about Welles. Bill, I have been thinking. How about my going to see Nasser? He would *have* to see me. You know, wife alone, worried, that sort of thing. I hate him for this, but I would even *beg* if it would help."

As my words tumbled over each other, I saw Bill and Samia exchange a glance and she slipped out of the room.

"No, Pat," Bill said in his soft, thoughtful voice. "Welles and I talked about that. We both think that you should stay away from the Egyptians." He smiled slightly, adding, "They don't respect women anyway, so let me tackle them. You concentrate on the foreign community. You know—embassy, private business, oil company people. All good friends of ours and they are really plugged in. First we have to find out what has happened, and they can help on that. *Then* we figure out what to do about it.

"And, Pat"—Bill's gentle voice was even more serious now—"the most important thing is to keep it quiet."

This surprised me and I looked at him quizzically. I thought that the greater the fuss we could make, the better. Nobody can expel a newsman without a reason, I thought. Give it a lot of publicity and they will have to back down. I was sure that if we embarrassed them enough we would win.

But right then Bill Landrey taught me a most important lesson. Being a warm and caring friend, he led into it slowly. He allowed me time to understand and accept.

"You haven't read anything about this in the papers," he began, "nor have you heard it on the news. And yet every newsman in this town has written the story because it is significant. They are all sitting on it, tight. Do you know why?"

I shook my head, honestly baffled. I had simply assumed that nobody knew about it except the perpetrators and us.

"When a newsman is in trouble with a foreign government, he has no overt friends. Everything must be done quietly, behind the scenes, without leveling blame. Right now the Egyptian government has several options: to enforce the order, to minimize it, or to rescind it and pretend it never happened. If the story gets out now, we force them to be rigid whether they want to be or not. They are pushed into a corner—by us, don't forget—and they would lose face by giving in. Then the expulsion would stand, and they throw the book at Welles.

"However"—he smiled slowly—"if we move fast and put quiet pressure on them from all sides, pressure that threatens them—economically, politically, in all directions—*without* publicity, they have room to reconsider and to decide that their own pique is not worth the price.

"If you crowd anyone, you lose," he continued. "We are going to hit this thing hard, and quietly. We are going to examine every idea from the negative view first: can it hurt? If not, we do it. And we are going to be just as cool and objective as we possibly can."

"And you know what, Bill?" I said, smiling, because I was right with him now. "We are going to *win!*"

"That's my girl," Bill said warmly.

And he concluded Lesson One with a kiss.

"The American Embassy can help, though, can't they?" I asked, neatly setting myself up for Lesson Two.

Bill shook his head slowly. "On the level we are talking about, yes. That is to say, quietly, in informal discussions. But they won't launch an official protest for many of the same reasons. And, frankly, for others too, which I don't quite agree with. American relations with the Arabs are tenuous and nobody wants to rock the boat. They will do everything they can behind the scenes, and that will be a lot. But whether we like it or not, no embassy is going to lock horns with its host country over one man."

My thoughts reverted to the three American businessmen, one of them a vice-president of the prestigious Bechtel Corporation, who had been murdered in Baghdad earlier that year. I recalled that the American Embassy had hardly said a word in protest.

"All right, Bill," I said, getting up. "Where do I begin?"

Ten minutes later I was on my way, carrying a list of friendly foreigners who had lots of clout. My banner unfurled, I charged off on my gallant steed.

Quietly.

13

The Dam Breaks

We seemed to be stuck in glue that whole first week. Bill hounded the Egyptian government offices but got nowhere. Others among our press corps joined in too, notably Charles P. Arnot of ABC, Frank Kearns who was then with CBS, and AP's talented Wilton Wynn who now writes for *Time*. But everyone drew blanks. Blanks accompanied by those slight flicks of the eyelid which are dead giveaways to any good newsman.

"Sure they know," Bill said, when the five of us were meeting in his office at week's end. "But no one wants to stick his neck out by telling us what's up. The pressure is building and they are beginning to run scared."

"Now is the time to hit it as high up as possible," chimed in Charlie Arnot. Then, turning to me, he asked, "How did it go with Norb today at the embassy?"

"He is really marvelous," I answered. Norbert Anschuetz was then deputy chief of mission at the American Embassy. "Their hands are tied, officially, of course. But he is making darn sure that the word is out," I continued, "and that kind of concern has got to bring results."

Frank Kearns spoke up then with the puzzle that had been troubling us the most.

"I still can't figure what they are accusing him of," Frank said, frowning. "They always give some reason for expelling a guy. Usually phoney, but *something*. I haven't heard anything at all on Welles, though. Have you?" he asked, looking at each of us in turn.

We shook our heads somberly.

"No," Bill said slowly, "and that is what worries me. It looks as if they are just out to get him, in any way they can. My hunch is that Welles' reports about Egyptian involvement with the rebels in Lebanon were hitting too close to home." He smiled at me and said, "Good reporting is a pretty thankless business. You get under somebody's skin and he wants you out, before it hurts too much."

"Poor Welles," I murmured, deeply troubled. "Sitting up there in Beirut not knowing what's going on. I can't get through by phone, but at least he knows what we're trying to do because I write him every day."

The men exchanged glances.

"Have you had a letter from him?" Wynn asked gently.

"No," I said slowly. "But I'm sure he is awfully busy . . ."

Bill cut in abruptly: "There is something you had better know, Pat. Your letters are not going out. You write them and mail them, but the farthest they ever get is into a cardboard carton in the censor's office. No doubt Welles' letters are winding up in the same place. They will sit around in the box for a couple of days until a minion scoops them up and puts them in your dossier. You will never see them again, either of you."

I was on my feet by this time. "But why? Those letters are of no earthly use to *them*. Why would they keep us from even writing to each other?"

"Baby, it's called harassment," Frank answered. "They are after Welles, and they want you both to be as unhappy as possible, hoping that you will leave and get out of their hair. If they *really* had anything on Welles, they wouldn't have to do it this way. They would simply say 'leave' and be done with it."

"Oh wow," I groaned. "Okay, I'll go. And happily. I'll join Welles in Beirut and stay with him until this madness is over. Then we can come back, together."

I checked my purse to see if I had my passport with me. Good, it was there.

"I'll go down and get my exit visa right now," I added, and started to leave. But Bill's next words stopped me in mid-stride.

90

"They won't let you go," he stated flatly. "That's the hell of it. Keep him out, keep you here . . . until he confesses to whatever 'sin' they finally come up with. Then the Hangens are condemned as spies or worse and sent packing. *Voila!* The honor of Egypt is redeemed, unsullied by vicious foreign reporting, clear for all to see."

"Oh, now wait," I exclaimed. "I simply can't believe that. Nobody could be that cruel."

Nobody said a word, but their faces made it plain. Clearly I hadn't been around long enough, but that afternoon I was to make up for a slow start.

They wished me luck as I left for the visa office, and they were still there to ease my dejection when I returned an hour later. The exit visa had indeed been refused. I was not to leave Egypt. I was to go home and await further instructions. And that, young woman, was that.

"I had to at least try," I said to my Four Wise Men as I rejoined their strategy session, "but I still can't believe it. I'll take your word for everything from now on, I promise." I shrugged wearily and asked, "So where do we go from here?"

It turned out that they had been hard at work discovering possible new pressure points during my absence and had assigned each of us tasks to pursue. And so a new week began.

It was right about then that I first noticed the man in the dark blue suit.

He was of medium height, slight, with a black mustache. Nothing outstanding about him. He looked just exactly like every third Arab you pass in any Cairo street. But that was the thing I finally noticed about him: *he never passed.* He was always there, in the corner of the picture. The one leaning against the wall reading a newspaper in the entrance to our apartment building; the guy sitting in the far chair in the corner of the hotel lobby; the last man to get on the streetcar, at the other end. Good God, I thought when he finally registered. This man has been at the edge of my retina for days. The same one. I am being followed!

I phoned Bill as quickly as I could, to tell him of my discovery.

I expected him to explode with indignation or else accuse me of paranoia. But Bill only chuckled.

"Your guy must be better than most if it has taken you this long to spot him," he said. "We all have tails, didn't you know? Mine has been around so long that we say 'good morning' and 'good night' to each other." Then he added: "You don't have to worry about him. He is just padding your dossier with daily reports. Actually you can have some fun if you want to. Try this." And he taught me a favorite indoor sport of foreign residents in the Middle East: the cigarette trick.

I tried it later in the lobby of the Nile Hilton. Pretending to be waiting for a friend, I carefully avoided looking toward the corner where I knew my blue suit was perched. Then with slow deliberation I took out a cigarette and searched my purse for a match. Blue suit was on his feet in a split second, hurrying to offer me a light! Bill was right: Arabs are so steeped in polite convention that they will even break their cover to comply. I thanked my little shadow who went in and out with me. But I couldn't resist saying, "See you around!"

And I did. Blue suit was everywhere, and now that we had met, his shadowing had all the subtlety of a right to the jaw. The only thing that disturbed me was when he got to where I was going *ahead* of me. Obviously my phone tappers were on blue suit's team and they really had me charted. But did they have to be so obvious?

My nerves were screaming "uncle" by this time. Welles had been barred from Egypt for nine whole days and we seemed no closer to getting him back than when it all started. Our press friends had been tireless in questioning officials but no one had come up with anything. The best I could do with my foreign contacts was to get promises that they would vouch for Welles' honesty as an objective reporter. It all seemed so slim, so non-productive, so slow.

But then, miraculously, the tenth day came and the dam began to break.

My telephone woke me that morning, so early that its ringing blended with the braying of donkeys plodding through Cairo's streets carrying their produce loads to market. The voice was low and deliberate, but indistinct to me because it was pre-coffee time.

"Yes, this is Mrs. Hangen," I managed, clearing my throat a few times. "I'm sorry, Mister who? Amed?"

Murmur, murmur from the phone. Then: "Mrs. Hangen, are you there?"

"Yes, yes, of course," I mumbled, shaking my head to clear the cobwebs. "You are Mr. Amed from the Ministry of Information. What? The minister wants to see *me?*"

I was up now, straight up beside the bed, bending over the telephone.

"At nine o'clock? In the president's office. Oh yes, yes, of course. *Yes.* I'll be there. Thank you. Thank you very . . ." But the phone clicked dead at the other end.

Dear God, I breathed, running a hand through my hair. The minister of information! This is *it.* We are either in or we're out. No more of this blasted limbo. We will be together, no matter where. Anything will be better than *this.*

I ran to turn on the tub. Then searched the closet for my best orange dress. Oh no! Still at the cleaners. Nothing to wear! Coffee. That's what I need. I raced to the kitchen, fumbled for the electric pot and spilled coffee grounds all over the floor. Got the thing plugged in, and then poured a glass of grapefruit juice. With its sharp sourness, I stopped flailing around . . . and finally woke up.

Must tell Bill, I thought and hurried back to the telephone. Then I noticed the clock. Only six-thirty? And here I am, hopping around like a toad in a hailstorm. Slow down, baby; let's think this one out, carefully.

It took the full two hours, but by the time I hailed a taxi at eight-thirty to drive to the Presidency I was calm and felt fairly well prepared to meet whatever I might have to meet.

Anything, that is, except the love-in that awaited me.

The minister's private secretary was watching as my taxi drove up to the austere Presidency gates. He bowed low as the gates parted, and smiled so broadly that it scared me. (My, what

93

big teeth you have, grandmother.) I would have felt much better had he snarled.

"Good morning," he gushed. "Welcome. It is good of you to come." He slid onto the seat beside me and directed the driver on through the garden. "The minister is waiting for you. You will have coffee? Tea? A beautiful day, don't you think?" And on and on. He reminded me of the Chipmunks in a recording session. But at least I didn't have to talk. I needed those moments to come up for air. His servility was smothering and I found it hard to smile. But smile I did. This was no time to alienate *anyone*.

As we pulled up before the towering old ochre building that was Nasser's official residence, its gilded front doors slowly swung wide. I felt like Ali Baba, and for a moment I hoped that I too would find an earthen jar to hide in. I was beginning to get nervous again and I prayed that whatever might happen, I would be able to handle it.

As it turned out I didn't have to do much of anything. The information minister greeted me effusively, begged my pardon for any inconvenience this trip might have caused, and offered me a chair.

"A little coffee perhaps, madame?" he began, a bit too affably, I felt, under the circumstances. "And a sweet to go with it? These are my favorite—Turkish Delight. I must share them with such a lovely lady."

Oh please, I thought, spare me this. Let's just say it, whatever it is.

But of course I remained silent. Smiling as warmly as possible, I choked down his sticky candy and waited.

Then: "Madame," the minister began in a serious tone, "I fear that there has been a little mistake. Your husband, ah, such a fine journalist, your husband. He has had some trouble, I hear. Something about returning to Egypt, to continue his brilliant work. Ah, so unfortunate"—his glance now sadly downcast, dusting the rug. "Such a pity that these things happen."

Little mistake! I could have thrown his bronze desk lamp straight at his sadly shaking head!

"But madame will understand of course," he continued, switching to a confidential tone. "There are so many in government who make errors. The president and I wish there were not such people, but what can we do?" His hands formed an open gesture of helplessness. "Possibly there are such people in your government too?" This, said with a smile implying confederacy. "Ah, but I suppose we must forgive them. They do not understand," he said, smiling into my eyes, "as *we* do."

Then I spoke. I had to, or drown in this collusive syrup.

"Mr. Minister," I said softly, "are you saying that Welles may return to Cairo now? That he is no longer expelled by your government? That we may continue to live here, and that he can work freely again?"

"Ah, my dear lady," he interjected, "you miss my point. Your good husband never *was* expelled. No, no. Just a nasty mistake. Such a shame to cause such misunderstanding among friends." He smiled sadly. "We like Mr. Hangen and we want him to be one with us. Please tell him for us."

"No, Mr. Minister," I said calmly. "*You* tell him. I really think that he would like to hear it straight from you. Because," I continued, unable to resist using his own *zusammenheit* right back at him, "*he* might not understand, as you and I do."

The minister rose. "Dear, dear lady," he said, kissing my hand, "such a pleasure. Of course, it shall be done, right away. And your husband will be back with you very soon."

"*Inshallah,*" I murmured as I went out the door. And I heard his voice echo my words, for in the Middle East no one dares to leave a declarative sentence hanging without protecting it with "God willing."

14

Learning the Ropes

There was nothing to do now but wait. Miserable word! Webster handles it easily: abstaining from action or departure till some expected event occurs. Clearly he was never there.

Waiting is pain in the absolute. Pure, unadulterated psychic agony in which each tick of the clock rebounds off the eardrum to make every nerve-end scream. Muscles knot tightly, tension floods one's entire nervous system. Pacing is no better than sitting, and watching at the window is plain masochism. There is neither letup nor relief. You are in for the duration and they have thrown away the key.

I spent the day in that prison of inactivity. Now in high anticipation, now distraught. What if something has gone wrong! Could the minister have changed his mind between bites of Turkish Delight? I would have phoned him except that I was loath to tie up the line if Welles was trying to get through.

Just as I knew for certain that we had been duped, the door flew open and Welles strode in, wreathed in smiles. He was positively radiant as he tossed his suitcase aside and entered the room.

"My darling, you *made* it!" And we were in each other's arms, clinging together. Then Welles held me away for a moment and we looked at one another in wonderment. He shook his head slowly and, with a gentle smile, held me closer still. It was true; we were really together again!

All of the grim details came out later, over our celebration dinner set in candlelight. Welles had been kept completely in the dark the whole time he was in Beirut. We might have forgotten him for all *he* knew, because none of our mail got through. The American Embassy was gracious but simply had no clue. He was completely alone, incommunicado, left in a void. Then two days ago a letter of mine, smuggled out in a friend's pocket, finally arrived and he no longer had to live on faith alone.

"There was enough love in that one letter to last a lifetime," Welles said. "It's all over now, though. The whole stupid thing is behind us. But the hell of it is, I still don't know what happened."

"Did you hear anything at all in Beirut?" I asked. He had spent his days talking to everybody and his brother there, just as we had here.

"Well, the Lebanese picked up one wild story," he began. "I had appeared, supposedly, on Baghdad television in a diatribe against Egypt and had personally hanged Nasser in effigy. Right there in front of the cameras. Can you beat that?" And he laughed, but hollowly.

"Don't tell me that anyone believed such nonsense," I replied with amazement. "In the first place, your reports only appear on American television. In the second place, you don't denounce anyone. And thirdly—"

"Yes, I know. I don't hang rag dolls either," he finished for me. "But no, the man who told me was amused by the whole idea. However"—his brown eyes were serious now—"it just might be the kind of thing these people would dream up. Any crazy story could get us out for good if they don't like my reporting."

Welles looked very thoughtful then. "I think," he said slowly, "that the information ministry here was all set to go with that Baghdad story. But the questions all of you were asking got high enough up to scare somebody. The president's men don't like to be irritated. So they called it off. It must have been close, though, or the Lebanese wouldn't have heard it." He shook his head and said, "I think that we almost had it."

"Welles, please, let's leave," I said then. "If they are going to be *this* impossible, why stay and take any more? There are lots of other places we can go—"

"Wait a minute, sweetie," he cut in. "This is no time to go *anywhere*. Let them think that they hounded us out? That we gave up? No, you don't mean that. That's not the way."

I nodded even though I would have given anything to leave Egypt right then and never come back. But of course he was right.

"Let's stay for now," he continued. "It is still a good story, you know, when we can dig through to it. We will stick it out for the time being, and leave on our own terms. Don't you think that's the best way?"

Yes, I did. But I didn't have to *like* it.

We lived in Egypt for more than a year after that. Our Cairo apartment was in the center of town on a wide thoroughfare called Kasr El-Nil. It is a busy street which cuts off diagonally from the Nile River and carries its crush of tooting cars, bicycles, produce-laden camels, donkey carts trimmed with jingle bells, and milling pedestrians through the modern city to Cairo's teeming market section. Our living-room balcony was ideal for watching this passing parade and I never tired of gazing down six stories into that animated chasm. Often I closed my eyes and tried to distinguish smells and sounds, testing my progress in understanding this curious world. Roasting chestnuts, almond blossoms, bus exhaust, camels, banked charcoal. Redolent mixture of the East, accompanied by an organ grinder's pie-plate tunes, a donkey's bray, the muezzin's lilting call to prayer from the minaret around the corner. And always honks, bell clangs, hawkers' chants, and tire squeals.

Welles' office was in the same building, three floors below our apartment. When we finished breakfast and he went down there to work, I often went exploring in the streets. Our building was built in 1953, as were most of the others lining Kasr El-Nil. They are built alike, of yellow-brown stucco, rising ten or twelve stories high and with no apparent architectural design. It was hard to tell them apart. To complicate things further for newcomers, they hide their addresses high in the eaves, so

98

only the most experienced can read them. Even the doormen "boabs" look alike, wearing long flowing *gallabiyah* gowns and white turbans.

This conformity was a by-product of the flurry of modernization that began with Gamal Abdel Nasser in 1952 and continues still. The ever-widening boulevards with planted islands; the rambling department stores that synchronize their white sales with January promotions in the western world; the shimmering tourist hotels that hug the river bank, and the interchangeable downtown apartment buildings.

Welles and I discovered exactly how confusing they could be when we were invited to have cocktails at the apartment of a casual friend. Literally casual: he warned that he might be delayed getting home, so we were to make ourselves comfortable if we got there first.

Sure enough, he wasn't at the door when we arrived, but the bowing servant welcomed us and ushered us into a softly lighted living room in which cocktail things were set out and a Brahms quartet was spinning on the record player. Welles mixed martinis while I sank into a chair by the phonograph and read the album notes.

We had just raised our cocktail glasses in a toast when a handsome Egyptian walked out of the bedroom, looked at us with surprise, then held out his hand in greeting. Welles shook the hand, murmured something about our host always being late, and asked the newcomer what he would like to drink.

Our companion was amused. His eyes twinkled and he said, "I'm afraid you have made some mistake. This is my apartment and I don't know your friend. But do stay," he continued as we exchanged embarrassed glances. "Some people are coming whom you might enjoy meeting."

I wanted to sink through the floor. Welles already had retrieved his jacket and was heading for the door. I splashed my martini on the coffee table in an awkward attempt to give it back, made a few passing jabs at sofa pillows to plump them again, and hurried after him. But our host, now greatly distressed, blocked the door.

"No, NO!" he said, his voice rising. "You can't go now. You are guests in my home."

The man looked distraught and his genial invitation had turned into an outright plea. Obviously he would be deeply offended if we refused his hospitality; the fact that we were strangers was of no consequence. Arab sensitivity is dictatorial; we turned back and sat down again.

At this, our host was all cordiality. He introduced himself as Ali, joined Welles on the sofa, and beamed expansively on us both as if we were his own inventions. Then he clapped for his servant to bring hors-d'oeuvres.

Welles excused himself and went to phone our bona fide host to explain our delay and ask directions. I stayed with Ali and told him how much we appreciated this unexpected kindness. Then in rapid sentences punctuated with flamboyant gestures, wide smiles, and offers of more drinks and canapés, Ali spoke about himself: he was a lawyer, a graduate of the American University in Beirut, a bachelor with four sisters to settle before he could marry, a weekend overseer of his family farm in the Nile delta, and an indefatigable political analyst. As is every adult male in the Middle East.

When Welles returned, we talked some more and then finished our drinks because we knew that we should be on our way.

"I wish you could stay to meet my friends," Ali said as we left him at the door. "But since you can't, I'll invite you again soon."

We had a new friend.

My first real friend in Cairo, however, was right in our apartment. His name was Moheiddin, a coal-black Nubian from the Sudan who cooked like a graduate of Cordon Bleu and kept house as I had always meant to. He had all the talents of Aladdin's genie. The silver and brass shone with polishing, our clothes were always neat and pressed, and invariably tea was served before we were even aware that we wanted it.

In addition to guiding our household with a firm hand, Moheiddin nominated himself my economic adviser. Which was sometimes a bit hard to take, especially at breakfast.

"Everybody cross with Nasser," he informed me one morning after Welles had left for work. I was having a second cup of coffee before facing the day and would have preferred peace and quiet, but he had something on his mind. A few half-hearted questions brought me the news that Cairo's cooks were up in arms because food prices were rising. This was Nasser's fault, in their view, because he had promised instead that costs would go down.

"But prices can't always go down," I said, trying to remember when bulls do become bears. And failing, just as I had failed elementary econ for the same reason.

"Nasser promised!" Moheiddin insisted.

It dawned on me that this lecture might have something to do with our household accounts. Just possibly our outflow of Egyptian pounds had hit the rapids. Since it is the custom in foreign homes to entrust the cook with marketing, Moheiddin was in charge of our exchequer. Friends had warned that I must go to the produce stalls occasionally myself, to keep our accounts in line with actual prices. So remembering their warning, I decided a market tour was indicated.

Moheiddin continued muttering grumpily about high prices. I debated whether or not to stuff him back in his lamp. Instead I tried to end the discussion by saying, "Well, people make more money now, don't they?"

That was exactly the wrong thing to say. I had left an opening as wide as a barn door, and he galloped straight in.

"I don't make more money," he grumbled, and wandered off to dust a book or two before coming back in for the kill.

Now I understood why my tutor always chose to open the classroom after Welles left for work. I was Moheiddin's pigeon and until I learned about Egyptian wiles, I would be plump and gorgeous game. I determined then and there to learn.

Cairo's main produce market is a block-square hive that could pass for any wornout stock show arena in America. Rickety wooden stalls crowd the floor space, leaving minimum passage for the hundreds of elbowing shoppers who daily throng to market. The counters are heaped with fragrant fruits and vege-

101

tables; moist piles of fish lie beneath hanging clusters of smoked eels in another part of the enclosure, and other counters bear portions of fish vertebrae covered with dried cracking skin. The fragrant and the fetid sealed in by a low domed ceiling. As I entered that close, airless shed, the smells were so overpowering that I wanted to forget the whole thing. But there was no choice: I was already moving with the tide. Tiny Moslem women veiled in black pressed into the small of my back, pushing me on. I felt huge and terribly foreign, and thought it best just to go along. Soon I became accustomed to the strange smells and my curiosity returned. First stop: the fruit stalls. Wonderful confusion of colors: apples, polished like red reflectors, piled on oranges piled on lemons, and all forming nests for bananas and soft golden mangoes. Squat woven baskets held strawberries. Smiling vendors offered samples, shouted inducements to buy, and swooped to retrieve those fruits which were knocked off the heap. It was bright and gay as could be, until I began to ask prices. Then market life became real and earnest.

"Your sign says fifteen piasters for strawberries," I began, addressing a swarthy vendor who had been shouting and smiling moments before, but who now appeared to shoulder all the cares of the world. "How many strawberries may I have for fifteen piasters?" I asked.

He looked at me solemnly, then reached forward and dipped his hand into the strawberry patch and brought up five of assorted sizes. He offered them to me. I shook my head.

With his free hand, my antagonist plucked one more berry from the basket and added it to his offering.

A pack of onlookers formed a semicircle behind me, peering over my shoulders, trying to cover giggles with cupped hands. They knew the game; I didn't.

All right, I thought. I've always been pretty good at sports and you don't scare me at all. I scooped up a handful of berries myself and, holding them out, I said, "Those *and* these, fifteen piasters."

Before I knew what had happened, the strawberries were wrapped in newspaper, shoved into my arms, and my piasters pocketed by the vendor who then turned his back. The crowd lost interest and dispersed as quickly as it had gathered. There was no point in my objecting on the grounds that I had only begun, because the game was over. So I wandered on among the stalls, calculating that my berries had cost about twenty-five cents each, and feeling very foolish. I had hoped that this excursion, when I reported it, would impress both Welles and Moheiddin, but as a bargainer I was a flop. Failure went to my head and I was no longer interested.

Then a melon vendor blocked my way, waving a ripe yellow melon near enough for me to smell its sweetness. He shouted, "One, lady! Only one!"

It looked lovely. Just the thing for lunch, and a delicious way to win back my self-esteem.

"Fine," I said. "But what do you mean, one?"

"One Egyptian pound," he replied. "Very good price." And he tried to lodge it in my free arm with the alacrity of all great swindlers.

Oh no, not again! Nearly three dollars for a single melon. I shoved it back at the vendor, dropped four strawberries in my haste, and pushed back through the throng toward the doorway. All right, Moheiddin, I thought. I give up. Food shopping is all yours.

In those last months, Welles spent much of his time away from Cairo, exploring the sandy reaches of Saudi Arabia, the Sudan, and many of the tiny oil sheikhdoms dotting the Persian Gulf, and I played Egyptologist while he was away and found endless enchantment. I climbed towering, narrow ladders to reach the slit entrances halfway up the sides of giant pyramids, and slid down dark passages into the burial tombs inside. I loved the Sphinx, although I never got used to its small size: pictures had been deceiving, and on my first visit I almost walked right by without noticing it. But most wondrous of all were the overnight boat rides up the Nile to Luxor and the storied Valley of the Kings. There one walks with Pharaohs and sups from lotus leaves. Aïda becomes flesh and blood because the stage set is real and perfectly preserved; imagination soars, and treading the ceremonial road of Ramses II, with its scores of life-sized lion honor guards, one becomes a queen.

I always went to the airport to meet Welles when he returned from his travels, which always seemed to be at three or four A.M., as if the planes were slipping in under cover of darkness to avoid detection. And they invariably sat out on the tarmac for several minutes while Egyptian health crews went aboard to spray the plane.

"Germs of revolution, do you suppose?" I whispered to Welles the first time this spraying occurred.

"Unh-unh," he murmured like a good conspirator. "Need guns for those. This is DDT. Must be for some innocent plague that only kills. Like typhoid."

"But you don't *spray* for typhoid," I said.

"No," he agreed, "but they've heard about the typhoid problem in the Persian Gulf. And the Egyptians operate on the theory that if it's bad, spray it with DDT. It's practical, because they happen to *have* DDT."

There is a wonderful cleanness about Cairo at dawn. Slightly damp with night dew. A soft taupe veil resting on vacant streets and on buildings whose blinds are closed in sleep. Donkey carts jingle their way into town from wakeful delta villages, crossing single file over Nile bridges, clopping along silent streets to the marketplace. Even the Nile is quiet with a hazy webbing of mist shifting lightly on its surface. Crude but extraordinarily graceful felucca sailboats follow the breeze downstream, but leave neither ripples nor wake as history, unreal as the Flying Dutchman. The soft, high notes of muezzins float in contrapuntal harmony with church bells, the scream of a camel, a donkey's bray. Then the air quiets again. Soon Cairo will awake.

We were always glad to be riding through town at this hushed hour. At rest, the city is beautiful, glistening as from a thousand scrub brushes. When she wakes, the transformation from still, clean beauty to shrill, sooty clutter is almost instantaneous. Cairo never stretches and yawns. She springs awake, bounds off in all directions, shouting out a cacophony of whines, grunts, screams. Every cell in her structure is wrenched into movement. Another convulsive day begins.

104

15

Let My People Go

The political climate in Egypt was deteriorating rapidly. It was 1960 and Nasser's sycophants had finally stuffed his ears so full of lies that he was deaf to the moans of his people. Secret police were everywhere; jails bulged with political prisoners; servants were bribed to lie about their employers, and paid informers searched private premises indiscriminately.

Worst of all for those of us who were trying to tell the story of Egypt's agony was the thick blanket of censorship that was slowly smothering us. News sources dried up. Within weeks it became impossible for journalists to work in Cairo at all, so one by one the foreign news bureaus closed and moved elsewhere. Correspondents who stayed had to shuttle to Beirut in order to file their stories. It became less and less worth the effort.

Coinciding with these events in Egypt, trouble was brewing along the border between China and India, and NBC decided that the time was ripe to open a news bureau in New Delhi. Welles was given the job and we were both delighted. All that we had to do was wind up our affairs in Cairo, pack our belongings, and leave. The sooner the better.

We booked passage on a German freighter scheduled to sail from Port Said in two weeks' time, to take us through the Suez Canal to the Red Sea, across the Indian Ocean, and on to Bombay. A fantastic journey: We were filled with excitement at the prospect and hurriedly began our preparations.

About five pounds of official documents were required of residents planning to leave Egypt in those chaotic days. The government told us exactly what to get, starting with a certificate from the information ministry that permitted us to take our household effects along with us. It was essential that all of our things accompany us to India because anything imported later would take months to clear customs. Every single picture, item of clothing, utensil, dish, had to have its own stamp. Then on to the bureau of censorship for approval of each book, phonograph record, even personal papers. All of this was in addition to the required exit visas and myriad legal documents, and we got them all.

It was five-thirty in the morning of sailing day when we started the long drive northeast to Port Said. We passed farmers in djellabahs rotating their primitive Archimedean wheels to force irrigation water from streams along the Nile delta; others, hardly clothed at all in anticipation of the sun which would soon sear their fields, goaded lumbering brahma bulls to keep their ploughs in the furrow. Then all was desert, flat arid sands broken only by an occasional palm oasis.

Suddenly something else: A line of ships appeared to be filing smoothly along that sandy horizon! We were approaching the Suez Canal, and from our lower vantage point the ships seemed to be sailing slowly across the sands. It was an enchanting desert mirage which gradually faded into reality as we neared the canal and entered Port Said.

We went first to the shipping line and got our tickets. Then, with our twenty pieces of hand luggage on groaning carts, we headed for customs. The remainder of our household effects, each piece individually wrapped, had been crated in a single mountainous lift-van which awaited us there. For each package we had stamped, certified, censored papers attesting to its contents and permitting its departure. Confident that the whole process of clearance would take only a matter of minutes, we entered customs at about ten that morning.

The first official looked dubious and took us to another official, who looked even more dubious, who took us to the chief of Port Said customs, who said, "No."

"No what?" we asked.

"No effects," he said.

"But why?" we asked.

"Just *no*," he said again.

"Now wait just a minute," Welles said then, fighting his astonishment. "We have all the correct papers with all the correct stamps. What do you mean, 'no'?"

Three hours later we were still arguing. The customs chief, whose name was Saleh, wanted to know how we came by these household effects in the first place. We explained over and over again that I had brought most of them with me when I came to Egypt for our wedding. My parents and I had sailed here for that very reason and had landed in Egypt at the Mediterranean port of Alexandria.

"Prove it," said Saleh. "Get me the record from Alexandria customs and I will let you go."

"But we can't get it now," Welles protested. "If we had known that you wanted it, we *could* have got it, but now it is too late because the ship sails tonight."

"Too bad," said Saleh, who was clearly all heart. "Without that paper, you can't take your things with you. I must leave now," he concluded, and he got up and walked out.

His deputy took over then and told us that if we could get the American consul in Port Said to swear to what we said, everything would be all right. Could we do that?

"You're damn right we can," Welles exclaimed. "You stay here. We will be right back."

We hurried to the American Consulate where our old friend Chester Beaman was in charge, explained our problem, and he straightaway gave us an official document of verification, complete with red ribbons and the American government seal. I had never seen anything more impressive than that shiny golden eagle and I was sure that our troubles were over. To make sure, Chester even phoned the deputy chief to vouch for us, and was told that we would be allowed to go.

We were joyous. Chester and his wife Mary invited us to their home for lunch after our final visit to customs. Jeanne and John Hogan were on their way up from Cairo, so we six could have a relaxing farewell party. Just one more trip to customs and we would have it made.

It was then about two o'clock. Welles and I went happily back

107

to the customs office and . . . found it closed. Right after Chester's phone call, the deputy had left and had sent *all* of his men home too.

For the next two hours we hunted people down. We finally found the deputy in the dunes of Port Said's swimming beach. A fat man with a bald head and a wide, sick smile. He was sitting in a lawn chair under an umbrella, in his beachrobe.

We pounced on him and presented our document proudly. He frowned. "This is not good enough," he said.

"What!" Welles exclaimed. "You *told* us to get this."

The inspector blinked and shook his head. "Not good enough," he said again.

We talked to him there on the beach for over an hour, and finally it was just too much for me. We were getting an obvious run-around without a clue to the reason, and I was angry.

"*Why* are you doing this to us?" I asked, my voice rising.

At that, Welles put his arm around me and said, "Nothing is worth your getting upset. The hell with the bastards!" And we left our fat toad blinking in the sun.

We went back to the consulate then. Welles phoned friends in Cairo who could put pressure on Chief Saleh, because we knew now that he had no intention of letting us take our things. By eight o'clock that evening we agreed that there was no hope. We were so numbed by that time that it almost didn't matter. We would cancel passage, return to Cairo, and try something else. But it was hard.

What happened? We never have known. Probably some Cairo official ordered Saleh to stop his harassment and to phone us, inviting us down. At any rate, he did and after much face-saving talk, at eleven-thirty we were finally permitted to leave with everything. We were loaded onto a barge with the lift-van and taken across the harbor in midnight blackness. The Hogans followed our pole-driven craft in a rented dinghy. Once aboard, we uncorked their bottle of champagne, toasted each other and roasted Saleh, until it was time to sail.

John and Jeanne lowered themselves back into the dinghy and we headed groggily off to bed. But as we rounded the narrow passage leading to our cabin, we heard John wail: "Wait! We are out of gas!"

Sure enough, their tiny craft was bobbing like an apple in a barrel, there in the murky waves beneath our stern. Our engines churned in the throes of departure, creating a hazard for the dinghy, as Welles ran and got a gas can from the crew. In the darkness he lost sight of the little boat but lowered the can in the direction of John's shouts. They connected.

We crawled into our berths, weak with exhaustion.

"There is no point in trying to tell anybody about this day," Welles said, "because nobody could believe it."

"You're right," I said with a tired shudder. "But now we know how Moses felt. And *he* would understand."

16

Come to the Show

The Indian weather bureau chalked up a record the day our ship reached Bombay. It was the heaviest monsoon rain to drench that west coast city in over a century. The sky was black fury, the harbor water a churning charcoal, and the driving downpour so dense that we couldn't even see the dock as we were tug-nudged toward our berth.

It eased briefly for our debarkation, and a fresh breeze brought the sweet smell of honeysuckle into the depths of the docks to welcome us. The wharf staff were eager to please and their smiles gave us such a sense of euphoria that we were able to take the customs inspector in stride when he waggled his head and asked:

"You are bringing with you a refrigerator *and* an air-conditioner?"

Welles nodded, perplexed.

"But you are allowed only *one* cooling machine," the inspector continued. "The book says so." He consulted a well-thumbed book of customs regulations.

"Refrigerators cool food," Welles said calmly. "Air-conditioners cool people. They are different. May I see your book, please?"

The inspector gave over his treasure. It was the official British customs manual of the year 1923. Nearly forty years old and still in use!

Welles explained gently that air-conditioners had not yet been invented when this book was written and therefore the rule could not possibly apply.

110

"Very well, then," said the inspector. "You are bringing one cooling machine, the refrigerator. Good. Now"—he gazed despondently at our long row of television equipment numbering fourteen pieces—"you are also listing *one* camera. I see many cameras. The book says just one."

It obviously distressed him to mention such unpleasantries, but he had a job to do.

"You are absolutely right," Welles said. "We are only allowed one camera. This *is* one camera. It has many parts because it is a highly technical television camera from America. Here"— he reached for the customs declaration—"this will take care of it." And he scribbled down a word.

"Excellent!" beamed the inspector. "Yes, you have one conglomerate camera. Oh, yes, that is fine."

He was so pleased to have avoided an argument that he signed our forms quickly and we were off.

The deluge hit again as we drove slowly into Bombay. Streets were completely awash and our taxi chugged along through fender-level lakes, followed by an old horse-drawn wagon carrying our lift-van. We had to stow the van in a warehouse before going on to our hotel, so we set off to look for the godown assigned to us. Our soggy little caravan ploughed through miles of drenched Bombay streets to get there. When we did, the godown was closed. No lights, no watchman, nothing. And the monsoon flowed on.

There was nothing to do but keep driving, hoping to find another warehouse that would take our giant box. We stopped at several but all were full. Then we saw one with its doors wide open.

"Just go on in," Welles directed the driver. "We'll ask later." And in we went—taxi, wagon, lift-van, all.

A small man in khaki workclothes hurried toward us from the rear of the godown, motioned us out.

"No, no! We have no room!" he shouted with agitation. "You must not come in."

But we were already inside and Welles had no intention of being turned away. His patience was about at an end.

"It is pouring outside," Welles said grimly. "And the box

111

leaks. Please let me talk to your manager." He sprang out of the taxi, not about to take no for an answer. Fortunately, the Indian manager turned out to be a very sad and very soggy Christian who had also been caught in the storm. He took pity on two other very sad and soggy Christians, and agreed to accept our dripping box for lodging. We gave him our profound thanks and splashed off through the waves to our hotel.

Bombay's Taj Mahal Hotel is a rambling gray stone structure topped by dozens of red-tiled cupolas and garnished with gingerbread, terraces, and arches. Inside, all rooms open off terraced walkways that surround deep light wells. Somerset Maugham once said that it looks like a jail, but to us the old place had immense charm. It was also dry and warm, and since we were thoroughly sodden from our first monsoon experience, we badly needed to be both. Hot baths, drinks and a relaxing dinner put our enthusiasm back in gear and we headed for bed with the idea of exploring Bombay in the morning.

When we rounded the catwalk leading to our room, I stopped Welles with a restraining hand.

"There is a man sleeping in front of our door," I whispered. "We had better tell the manager quickly."

But Welles only laughed and pulled me toward our doorway.

"Good evening," he said to the small man curled up on the doormat. The man leaped up, hastily straightened his white tunic, and saluted in great confusion.

"Memsahib, Sahib," he began, "I am very sorry to be sleeping. It will not happen again. I am here to take care of you. Anything you wish, you are please telling me. I will be here, always."

And he was. It was my first meeting with an Indian bearer, and I was soon to learn that there are no more ingenious problem-solvers than these modest men servants. But I never got used to stepping over one, asleep, every time I opened a door.

Our arrival in Bombay coincided with the first general election India had staged in five years, the third since her independence. Some fifteen thousand candidates were jeep-hopping through villages, leading brass bands around city suburbs, trekking up mountain paths to paste their poster portraits on tree trunks and bullock carts. Children serpentined through streets in campaign processions and poets composed eulogies. With no radio campaigning allowed, and no television possible, it was strictly a matter of personal appearance.

Two of India's most colorful politicians were in Bombay just then, contesting a parliamentary seat from that district. It was good fortune to begin Welles' new assignment with this view of Indian politics in microcosm, so we set off enthusiastically the next day along the campaign trail.

V. K. Krishna Menon, India's acerbic defense minister, was fighting for his political life against the highly respected Acharya J. B. Kripalani, an elder statesman from the opposition party. It was a harsh contest between two old pros and the big issue was Communism.

The sun was shining again. Before searching out our candidates we took a tour of Bombay and were enchanted by the lushness of this flowering peninsula, surrounded on three sides by blue bay and dotted with the bright red flame trees which shade the streets. Downtown boasts staid nineteenth-century British office buildings interspersed with leafy foliage, and all streets ramble toward the bay or climb up Bombay's scenic hills. A handsome city, until you arrive in the mud and cardboard hut areas where most of the population resides in barefoot filth and abject poverty.

In one such area we found our first political rally. It was for Krishna Menon. He was there, squatting cross-legged on a platform in the middle of a vast sea of people lounging on the ground. Lesser politicians crowded the platform with him. Menon sat dozing. He neither moved nor spoke.

"He is completely exhausted," I whispered to Welles. "I never saw a more helpless man in my life!"

"You will never see a better organized rally either," Welles said, watching the crowd as the speeches went on. "The behavior of these people is perfect, *too* perfect. Look at all those proctors! Each in charge of his group, like a grammar school at recess. It's about as spontaneous as choir practice."

Welles helped me to spot those Menon henchmen, and indeed they were everywhere: tall young men wearing badges of authority who cuffed the disorderly and prodded the sleepy. They produced cheers or silence, on order. In this land of bustling, joggling humanity the effect was eerie. When the meeting ended, Menon was lifted to his feet and helped out. We left too and raced for our car to join his caravan, some twenty cars, speeding through narrow, clogged mud streets at sixty miles an hour, heading for the next precinct rally. We followed them five times and at each rally we found the same organization, the same frightening calm.

Krishna Menon spoke only once. It was painful to watch. He clutched the microphone for support, spoke in a gravelly voice, and looked on the point of collapse. His words could have meant nothing to his hearers, since he spoke in English, and there was no sound from the huge crowd before him until the proctors signaled for applause or chants. This brought pandemonium, ceasing as abruptly as it began.

The Indian Communist Party supported Menon in this election, but we had not realized that the party was actually running the show. Menon's campaign manager, who was always at his side, was also head of the Soviet-Indian Friendship Society, the party's cultural mask. So order was the rule, and order they had. Lifeless, comatose, just like the candidate.

"Let's go find Kripalani," Welles said then. "I've seen about enough of this, haven't you?" And he started off, making a path for us through the crowd.

I hurried to keep up with his long-legged stride, not wanting to get lost in *this* mob. Wanting really to go straight back to the hotel and forget about the whole thing.

"Do we *have* to see any more, honey?" I asked.

Welles gave me a reproving look and said, "We would be covering only half of the story if we stop now. If you don't want to come with me on these things, just say so. You can stay at the hotel any time you like." And he turned on his heel and headed for the car.

Oh come on, I thought. I'm tired of this and you must be too.

114

We race around half the night in mud and filth, and for what? What good does it do?

Welles unlocked the car and held a door open for me to get in. I did. He went around to his side, slid behind the wheel, and started the motor.

"We have one hour left for Kripalani before the campaign ends," he said tersely. "We can talk about *this* later." And off we drove.

It took about fifteen minutes of searching through dark neighborhoods to find the Kripalani rally. Welles was preoccupied and I depressed. We were silent all the way.

The Menon rally had attracted a huge crowd, but this one had a carnival air: relaxed, noisy, sloppy. We were greeted with cries of "welcome" when we approached, and our way was made by a group of Kripalani supporters who urged us to the front. We took places in the crowd before the platform and waited. I began to find it exciting in spite of myself.

Towering over the crowd, a gaunt Indian Cicero in flowing white robes, Kripalani spoke Hindi in clear, resonant tones. The audience waved, shouted, and cheered him all the way. His words were largely anti-Communist, condemning Menon for his party ties. The crowd loved him and the old man appeared to reciprocate that affection. He concluded his speech with a ringing crescendo, and the words, "Beware of Communism!"

At that precise moment a siren sounded over the crowd, and all was still. It was midnight. By Indian law the campaign was over, including the cheering. Like the final gun at a football game when you know your team has lost, there was nothing further to do but go home. For Kripalani did lose, as they all knew he would. The unpopular Krishna Menon had the backing of Prime Minister Nehru and his strong Congress Party in addition to the Communists. Nehru had even threatened to resign if his friend were defeated, so the die had long since been cast. And the margin was nearly 150,000 votes.

"You were right," I told Welles as we got back in the car. "That wonderful old man is something else. I wouldn't have missed hearing him for anything."

Welles smiled and pressed my hand.

"I thought he might be," he said. "But you never know. He could have been just as moribund as Menon. That's why you have to be there, to find out."

17

Goa, Goa, Gone

Those were times of high hope for India. Prime Minister Nehru was still holding his divergent peoples together with his special charismatic glue, America was funneling vast amounts of aid money into the economy, and Russia was building prestigious hydroelectric plants for power and irrigation.

New Delhi's bright young men and women were filled with optimism. The air was charged with excitement and dinner tables were vibrant with talk of plans and prospects. We made our home in that capital city, and the Indian, British, and American friends we found during those early months remain valued friends to this day.

For the first several weeks we lived in Claridge's Hotel while we tried to find a home and an office. So many foreigners and Indians were moving into the capital that it was hard going. New Delhi's city planning sends all main streets shooting out from Government House like spokes from the hub of a wheel. At the far ends of those spokes are residential areas and we searched there, but Welles' news bureau had to be right in town; and apart from the huge old Raj-style government buildings, there were no offices at all. Nothing stood higher than one or two stories, including the shops in Connaught Circus. The term "downtown" was a euphemism for that single circle of stores, but that was all that New Delhi had and no one seemed to miss more pretentiousness.

We did, however. It is hard enough to move into an office and set up a news bureau, but converting somebody's house into one is something else again. The little stucco two-story we settled on was right downtown, but it had its drawbacks: the landlady lived on the ground floor with two grown sons, their wives, five grandchildren, and three big dogs. Welles' office upstairs was a single room large enough for two desks and a watercooler, and a bathroom with just the right-sized shower stall for his file cabinets. It wasn't perfect, but it *was* quiet when the grandchildren were in school and the dogs asleep. The encircling wisteria vines gave it a sense of peace, and it was within walking distance of the broadcasting facilities in town.

Finding our home was harder. Real estate agents were very good at locating empty houses, but they were never around when it came to negotiating, and we found that dealing with Indian landlords was a whole new ballgame. There were two houses that interested us right off the bat. Two smiling landlords promised to hold them for us, but while we were deciding between them, two other families signed leases and moved in. We learned quickly then. It's cash on the barrelhead that keeps those smiles from fading.

Most New Delhi houses have two stories, flat roofs, and a garden. One family occupies the ground floor and has use of the garden, while another has the second floor with additional space on the roof and, often, a fenced-in roof garden with canopy to protect it against the sun. Those roofs are pleasant in the evening when fresh breezes cool the air, but we wanted a ground-floor flat and the luxury of stepping out into our own garden.

We finally rented a place in Sunder Nagar, a quiet section where the houses all face rectangular grassy "maidans." Flamingo trees, lilac, and wisteria shaded our garden, and we often pulled cane chairs out into the evening fragrance. It was a pleasant home, made even more pleasant by our Madrasi cook-bearer, Robert. He was a slim young Christian with short black hair and a trim mustache, who cooked good Western meals as well as curries, and kept house beautifully. He also did our grocery shopping because he could get better prices than I. Even more important, he was always quietly cheerful. The only thing that bothered me about Robert was his adamant refusal to sweep.

"Cook-bearers don't sweep, Memsahib," Robert said politely when I first broached the matter. "My wife will help with dusting and polishing, and she will do the wash. But I will find you a sweeper."

"There are only two of us in our family, Robert," I said. "I couldn't handle the shopping and tradesmen and other new customs without you. But we don't need more people to help in the house."

"My wife is a fine baby-amah too, Memsahib," Robert continued, "for when the family grows. But I will hire you a sweeper."

His mention of a baby threw me for a moment. We wanted a family very badly but our luck had not been good: dozens of doctor's appointments and two miscarriages. I had been assured that there was no reason to worry, but I couldn't help it. And I felt uncomfortable when others brought it up.

"All right, hire a sweeper," I said, more to end the conversation than because I agreed. "But it will be your responsibility to see that he does a good job."

From that day on, we had an immaculate and happy home. Although the staff outnumbered the family, that was India, 1960. It was the way things were done.

It took some time to settle in because our furniture had to be made for us, but eventually our home was organized and we began to enjoy the relaxed atmosphere of New Delhi.

It was a friendly city, probably because no one had roots there, any more than we. So all its residents were transplants, with none of the old family snobbishness of Bombay or Calcutta. They were intelligent and charming too, for the capital attracted the best of the barrel.

We had been living in India for over a year when something happened that made us forget even the intense, overpowering heat. I finally was pregnant! After all our troubles in the past, now, this time, I was certain. Sister Cecile confirmed the wonderful fact in a Holy Mary examination room. The little nursing sister was almost as happy as I, and she embraced me lovingly as if I were her own daughter.

Welles was beautiful during the days that followed. He was tender and loving, and we found a new degree of closeness, compounded, I suspect, of an enormous sense of pride in each other. Just see what we can do! We felt so ebullient that we all but competed in trying to please. But when I took to making flaming desserts, which we both detest, we agreed that we had gone too far.

Then the mother superior of Holy Mary Hospital telephoned. She had been away on a trip and wondered if I could come to see her the following day. I was so euphoric that I could hardly wait to meet the woman who directed my splendid hospital.

I was in her office early the following morning. She had my file in her hand. It didn't take long.

"I am sorry, Mrs. Hangen," the mother superior began. "Sister Cecile loves people too much. Or, too *simply* would be more accurate, I suppose. She wants everyone to be happy. So I am afraid that she tells them what she thinks they want to hear."

Mother superior smiled sadly. "Sister doesn't mean any harm. But she hurts people cruelly sometimes . . . just as she has now hurt you. You are not pregnant, my child. I wish that I could say otherwise. But with God's help, one day you may be. God bless you."

It was all over, just like that.

I left the hospital in dreadful dejection. So it had happened again. I wanted so desperately to have Welles' child, and once again I had failed. Everybody in the world has children. Look around. They're all over India! Why not me? And how, oh God, *how* will I ever tell Welles?

Rounding a curve along the way home, upset and deep in thought, I didn't even see the five Indian bicyclists riding abreast in the road ahead. I was not aware of them at all until I was right on top of them.

The hand of God alone helped me to veer off, a split second before hitting them, and they scattered like chickens all over the road.

I was conscious of horrified faces and raised clenched fists reflecting in my rearview mirror as I sped on. And in that instant I was overcome by the enormity of my action and braked to the curb. There, stricken with remorse for everything, I fell forward on the steering wheel in a spasm of anguished tears.

But I didn't have to tell Welles after all. He knew from my face, the minute I walked in the door at home. He took me in his arms and simply held me.

"It's all right, sweetheart," he said softly. "Next time we'll make it certain." And we stayed that way for many moments, comforting one another but saying nothing.

By that time our infatuation with all things Indian had cooled considerably. Then, in 1962, it ended altogether with their invasion of Goa.

That little Portuguese enclave on the west coast had been a benign mole on India's thigh for over four hundred years: quiet, lethargic, harmless, smaller than Rhode Island, with a population of only six hundred thousand. But it faced the Arabian Sea and had the best natural harbor on the coast.

India abhorred another country's sovereignty over what she considered her soil, and the large sums of hard currency the Portuguese earned by exporting iron ore were galling. So the insult had been festering for years. Now, with increasing threats from China along the northern border, the Indian government needed to divert attention from that ominous scene while pondering a course of action. What better time, then, for picking on little Goa?

A plan was hatched in the mind of Defense Minister Krishna Menon to appropriate this piece of desirable real estate. But because the Indians prided themselves on nonviolence, Menon knew that they could not resort to open force.

"They have to make it look as though their hand is being forced," Welles explained. He was packing his bags again, and I was perched on his bed trying to follow the plot. Clearly I was not being invited to this war and I had to find out why.

"As I understand it," he continued, transporting an armload of shirts from dresser to bed, "a party of Indian border police will enter Goa and some will allow themselves to be captured. The rest will fall back and give the alarm. Then," he continued, well into the underwear drawer, "a smallish force will move in on the pretense of rescuing the captured guards and engage the Portuguese. Then comes the main force, and *voilà*, Goa is overrun. Menon will scream 'provocation' and that will be the end. How's *that* for hypocrisy?"

"But what about Nehru?" I ventured, still romanticizing that grand old man. "Surely he won't let them do anything so devious."

Welles shrugged. "He rebuked them for plotting without his permission, so the scenario may change slightly. But they will do it some way."

Suits and ties were in, and he snapped the suitcase shut, saying, "Menon is a crafty old devil, don't forget, and can make black look pure as the driven snow. They are lifelong friends and Nehru trusts him."

"With such friends," I quoted, "who needs enemies? I feel sorry for Pandit-ji."

"Don't," Welles countered. "He is a great man but he *is* a politician."

Welles grounded me, as I knew he would, largely because of transportation. India's cold shoulder toward Goa barred direct flights, so access had to be via the Karachi airport in Pakistan. He would use that route to enter Goa, but if his hunch was correct, the way out again might be difficult.

"So hold on here, if you will," Welles said. "This really shouldn't take very long."

And it didn't. Menon urged his security officers to step up subversion against the Portuguese. Indian border police trained saboteurs and slipped them into Goa. Newspaper headlines throughout India screamed "border provocation" over stories fabricated by the government. Tales circulated of oppression and terrorism in Goa and of heavy reinforcements of Portuguese armed forces. There were even reports of Portuguese raids into India.

Alone in New Delhi, I didn't know how much of this to believe, and I began to think that Welles might have got himself into a real cul-de-sac shooting match this time. But right then I received his first letter.

He had arrived late at night at Goa's Dabolim airport after a tedious flight from Karachi. It was a twenty-mile drive through coconut plantations to the capital city of Panjim and, contrary to the reports we had been receiving in Delhi, he saw only one armed guard outside the airport and two rifle-bearing civilians checking traffic on the primitive ferry that plies the river between airport and town. Thatch-roofed huts amid tall coconut palms were dark under a cloudless tropical sky. All was utterly peaceful.

"To give you an idea of how truculent the Portuguese are," Welles wrote, "I am enclosing a television report we did for the 'Today' show. The narration is mine. I think you can imagine what the film looks like."

I tore open both sides of the envelope to free the thick script. These narratives always fascinate me because they are transcriptions of the soundtracks on films. By speaking his narration right there at the scene of the story, the newsman is actually editing the film. His own words select segments for use, making a cohesive story from countless feet of news film. It requires fast, sound judgment for an effective account. And Welles is a master of both.

I unfolded the script and began to read.

For a beleaguered outpost under threat of imminent invasion, Goa is the most lethargic backwater I have seen. The mañana atmosphere hangs heavy over the sun-drenched, tile-roofed little capital of Panjim where the tempo of life hasn't changed since the Portuguese arrived early in the 16th Century. . . .

It will take a miracle to save Goa if India decides to invade. India's British-built Vampire jet fighters roar over Goa almost daily, and her new aircraft carrier has been sighted off the coast. All along Goa's 180-mile land frontier tough, turbaned Sikhs and other Indian troops are encamped.

Against this, the Portuguese offer a kind of Gilbert and Sullivan collection of antique weapons wielded by a tiny handful of men. Faced

123

with such a massive threat, almost any other people would reinforce or get out. But not the Portuguese.

They have an anachronistic kind of bravado mixed with fatalism. They are ready to tilt at Indian tanks with ancient muskets and World War I scout cars. The solitary frigate of the Portuguese High Seas Fleet that guards Goa may never land a shot on the enemy but it's ready to go down heroically. . . .

So there is a sort of tense lethargy in Panjim, Goa's vest-pocket capital of 50,000 inhabitants. People try to send their savings to Lisbon, but no one is building bomb shelters. At police headquarters everyone rushes to the balcony to watch Indian jet fighters hurtle overhead. Then everyone goes back to discussing the exploits of Vasco da Gama. In Goa the past is contemporary.

I folded the script and went back to Welles' letter. At the end he mentioned an Indian hand grenade attack on a Portuguese military post thirty-five miles inside Goa, and said that he and other Western newsmen planned to drive up that jungle road the following day to investigate. I was sorry he had included *that.*

Then came the story.

The newsmen had hired a taxi to take them to the outpost, which they found deserted, and they decided to push on toward the border. They wanted to see for themselves how much of an Indian buildup there might be, since they saw no Portuguese troops at all.

Several hundred yards still inside Goan territory they came upon Indian troops in company strength who had already hoisted their tricolor flags. There were sandbagged bren-gun posts set up, and heavily armed foot patrols were making forays into the Goan countryside. Welles and his colleagues were taken into custody at gunpoint. After prolonged questioning by an Indian paratroop captain, they were allowed to return in their taxi to Panjim.

The captain's final words as the correspondents drove off were, "Maybe we will meet there soon."

That night the full-scale invasion was launched. The Indian Army advanced on all sides with no resistance, and by noon

124

turbaned Sikh paratroops shouting *"Jai Hind"* had occupied the capital. Some Goan Hindus joined in those "Long Live India" demonstrations, but most residents hid fearfully behind closed doors. All Portuguese citizens were concentrated in Panjim under Indian guard, and many Portuguese police, the pallbearers of their empire, had tears in their eyes as Indians took quick control of the central police station.

Then came the end. Portuguese police hung out the white surrender flag at Panjim that night about fifteen hours after the attack began. The acrid smell of burning official papers at the governor-general's palace was the last whiff of Portuguese presence in India.

Communications had been knocked out early when Indian planes bombed Goa's transmitters, so there was no way for newsmen to get the story out. Short, that is, of getting out themselves.

Welles and two others blazed a trail back to India by road, in stages. Their first car broke down under the strain of negotiating crude by-passes around bridges dynamited by retreating Portuguese. They managed the next stage in an Indian government car and the last lap by ancient taxi. In spite of all that, they were the first newsmen to report directly on the Indian takeover of Goa.

18

Himalayan Hypocrisy

The little Portuguese mouse, as Nehru called Goa, had succeeded in eclipsing the elephant of Chinese Communist expansionism along India's border for a long time. But now the diversion was over and facts had to be faced.

For eight years the Chinese had been surveying and building roads through the Himalayan mountains bordering India. Their object was to connect Chinese Sinkiang with vanquished Tibet in order to tighten China's control over that proud, forgotten land.

But when the roadwork was completed, India woke up to the fact that she had a Chinese military highway going straight through her territory on the Aksai Chin plateau.

Prime Minister Nehru was caught by surprise and, with the connivance of Defense Minister Menon, decided to withhold the shocking news from Parliament and the nation. Then a second highway was blasted through the same area by Chinese troops, and check posts pushed deeper into Indian territory.

The two Indian leaders dodged and parried when Parliament began to ask questions. Nehru dismissed the seventeen-thousand-foot Aksai Chin plateau as a wasteland "where not even a blade of grass grows." Menon said soothingly, "There is no active hostility." And the Chinese came further into India.

In April 1962 Welles asked Defense Minister Menon about the border menace, and he seemed as sanguine as ever. They met in the book-lined sitting room of Menon's New Delhi home. The minister was slumped on a couch drinking black tea.

126

"The Chinese know they can't wage war against us," he said, stifling a yawn, "any more than we can against them. They fear losing prestige in a border settlement."

He flicked his tapered manicured fingers in the air as if to dispose of a bothersome gnat.

"That frontier has not been policed, as some people make out," Menon continued. "It is rather like the frontier between Canada and the United States. We hope that neighborly relations will prevail."

But just six months later China hurtled across the Himalayan border in a massive predawn attack on India.

The vast assault might have been avoided had India continued to look the other way. But China's nibbles were beginning to hurt. Nehru was sure that Russia would constrain the Chinese if they made trouble, so he dispatched Indian troops into that craggy terrain with orders to stand their ground. The impasse had become a simple matter of Indian self-respect.

India's defenses proved hopelessly inadequate, and nobody came to help. With over half the army away on the border of Kashmir and Pakistan, and the rest ill-equipped, they were unable to halt the Chinese troops who were plunging like rapids through mountain passes, spraying down toward the Indian plains.

Two days after the story broke, Prime Minister Nehru addressed the nation.

In weary tones he cautioned against panic and said, "Whatever may befall us in the future, I want you to hold your heads high."

"High, indeed! Seems they have lost their heads completely," Welles observed as he switched off the radio. "Nehru vacillates from arrogance to panic and nobody knows what to do. Russia hasn't come through, so now they are asking help from us."

"Will we help, do you think?" I asked, remembering Nehru's reluctance to deal openly with the West.

"With airlifts probably"—Welles shrugged—"but no active support. Who wants to fight China? No, we would be crazy to come in on this one."

We did, though: with mortars, recoilless rifles, and other automatic weapons. General Paul Adams, commander of a U.S. strike force, was even at the front. But by that time, as we were to see, it had become purely academic.

New Delhi was deep in shock those days. A state of emergency was declared, but with the exception of scattered demonstrations and much backroom political maneuvering, the city appeared as pastoral as ever. Several days went by before anything at all was done. Then frantic instructions went out to dig air-raid trenches, organize blackouts in border towns, marshal village militia, and give every able-bodied citizen rifle training.

Welles' bags were out again. This time he was packing for the eastern war front. We had just come back from checking the latest developments in town.

"The town is so quiet it's spooky," I said. "I don't like the looks of those air-raid trenches either. One good rain and we'll all be mud pies."

He grinned. "If you get an air raid while I'm gone, just stay home. Those shelters are about as well hidden as the Taj Mahal. Hey, where are you going?" he asked as I jumped up and started out of the room.

"To get my bag too," I said with a shudder. "You aren't going to leave me alone here with only mud holes for protection. I'll take a good gun battle any day."

"Honey, calm down!" Welles put his arms around me. "Nobody is going to bomb New Delhi. They just dug those holes to give people something to do. This isn't an air war, you know. Nobody is using planes."

"Welles, that's not the point," I argued. "I'd much rather be *with* you no matter where it is."

"I know," he said softly. "I really do. But this time I have no idea where we'll be. We may be on the move all the time. I just *can't* take you with me. Please understand."

He is right, Patrish, I said to myself. This war front is no place for you. And you're wrong to upset Welles now. He'll have enough on his mind without worrying about you. Don't let him go off this way. Come on! Be fair!

128

So I said, "This town is so eerie, I guess I let it get to me for a minute. I'm all right, really."

Then suddenly I knew the way. For both of us.

"Do you know what, honey?" I said, hoping that I sounded enthusiastic. "While you're gone, I think I'll do some stories about what's going on right here. Gordon Pates would like that, don't you think? And it will keep me too busy to worry about you." Then I smiled up at him and added, "Well . . . almost."

"Baby," Welles said, closing his bag, "did I ever tell you that I love you to pieces? I'm the luckiest guy in the world."

Then he kissed me and was gone.

I did start to work after Welles left that day. There was a lot going on in New Delhi, and although most of it was sadly ridiculous, it made good reading. Gordon Pates, then foreign editor of the San Francisco *Chronicle*, had asked for stories from time to time, and it was fun to be writing again. But . . . *of course* I worried.

Welles and his television crew were in Tezpur, the site of Indian Army Corps headquarters in the east. It should have been safe enough except for one thing: the day after they arrived, Tezpur gave up without a fight. It was a scramble to get out ahead of the Chinese troops who were advancing relentlessly down into the plains. As the Indian Army dissipated, so did Welles' purpose in reporting their actions. Very soon he came back home.

Then Krishna Menon called a press conference.

The hall in the Vigyan Bhawan was jammed. Each reporter opened a thick blank notebook, pencil poised, as the defense minister entered the room. This would be his first interview since the invasion.

Menon's hawkish features were grim. He declined a chair, stood straight, and looked at the press corps with undisguised disdain.

"The Chinese may come as far into India as they like," he said coldly, without emotion. "We are unable to stop them."

And he turned on his heel and left!

For a moment we sat in stunned silence. Then every reporter

129

jumped up and raced for the door. India had capitulated. *This was a story!*

Then came the perfect squelch: China declared a cease-fire. If she had been dazed before, this put India out for the count. At first no one believed it: just another Chinese trick. The old torturing drip-drip-drip. But no, it was true. They simply stopped, packed up, and went home. Leaving enough force to hold their uncontested 14,000 square miles of Indian land. A shaken, humiliated India went back to business as usual, and we felt that we had earned a vacation.

Actually newsmen never take vacations. When your profession is observing life and the whole world is your shop, there is just nowhere left to go. So you choose a place where interesting things are happening, pad it with side trips, and count on a great vacation.

The foreign ministers of India and Pakistan were meeting in Karachi right then to discuss the fate of Kashmir. President Ayub Khan was in Rawalpindi pondering his role in the negotiations. So we headed for Pakistan and figured that the holiday padding would be to wander through the Kipling country of the north.

Welles had arranged a television interview with President Ayub so we went directly to Rawalpindi, the sleepy little town on the Himalayan slopes which was then his mountain capital.

As we drove up the wooded hills north of town and approached Ayub's palatial white mansion, we were awed by the spectacular view. A breathtaking stretch of Kashmir mountains unfolded, a twenty-thousand-foot height of snow-covered grandeur.

"Now I understand why Ayub wants Kashmir," I said, marveling at the sight. "It's right there in front of him all the time. What a glorious temptation."

Welles agreed. "He is a mountain man anyway. He would rather be surrounded by fir trees and high peaks than anything. That's why he made this his capital. And, as you say"—he chuckled—"it is about as close to Kashmir as he can get."

"Will Pakistan get Kashmir away from India, do you think?"

130

I asked, remembering that the population of that beautiful state is mostly Moslem although India claims control of it.

"They've been arguing about it for fifteen years," Welles said, shaking his head. "They both want the vale especially, the lush productive part. But India won't give it up."

President Ayub greeted us graciously when we entered his sitting room. He and Welles had been friends for years but this was my first meeting with the distinguished army officer, trained at England's Sandhurst Academy, who was now chief of state. And I was quickly enchanted.

Ayub was not a tall man, but his military bearing made him seem so, and his presence commanded the room. Welles had told me what a charmer he was, but I was not prepared for his warmth and naturalness.

We all talked comfortably for a while and then the two men decided to start their filmed interview and I was moved into a corner to watch. The president offered me a cigarette, lighted it, and said that he hoped I would be comfortable. If I had known how to purr, I would have.

Then the camera began to roll.

President Ayub expressed himself in his usual forthright terms on a variety of subjects, including the Kashmir dispute. The surprise came when he spoke of Pakistan's readiness to put aside discussion of the treasured Vale of Kashmir and concentrate instead on who should control the rest of the former princely state. He thought their claim would prove substantial and that the vale would fall into their laps later, of its own weight. It was a clever tack and Ayub's words were the first inkling anyone had of it.

Welles was excited as we left the sprawling white mansion. "We have a real beat this time, sweetie," he exclaimed. "It's the first time they have ever considered side-stepping the vale." He laughed and shook his head. "Ayub is no dummy. It just might work."

"I hope so," I said dreamily. "If the vale were mine, I'd *give* it to him. I don't know when I've met anyone more impressive."

Welles glanced at me and laughed again. "Yep, he's quite a

131

man. Where did you put the stub of that cigarette?" And he laughed even more when I opened my purse and took out my Kleenex-wrapped memento.

The trouble started when Welles went to interview Foreign Minister Zulfikar Bhutto and mentioned President Ayub's remarks on Kashmir.

The foreign minister was clearly upset. He appealed to Welles to ask NBC not to use the story until after the next round of talks with India. Welles agreed. NBC had no interest in torpedoing international negotiations for the sake of a news beat. Bhutto expressed his deep gratitude, excused himself, and said that he would be right back.

Mohammed Sarfraz, Bhutto's public relations man, was with him when he returned to the office.

"No need to withhold any part of the film," the foreign minister said jovially. "You can use it anytime."

"Fine." Welles smiled, surprised. "I appreciate that, Mr. Minister. Thank you very much." Then he frowned. "I would like to air-freight the undeveloped negative to New York right away, but I will need a customs clearance."

"No problem," Bhutto assured him. Then, turning to Sarfraz, he said, "Kindly facilitate the shipment in every way."

"Certainly," replied the public relations man. "I shall be standing by to do whatever is required. Shall we say three o'clock at my house? Good."

That gave us two hours to type scripts, package films, and get the shipment ready. The airline cargo office was open until five, so Sarfraz would have ample time to help with our clearance. Then we would ship the package ourselves.

At three o'clock we rang his doorbell, but nobody answered. The house was deserted. No message. Nothing.

How do you find someone in a strange town if he doesn't wish to be found? We had become very experienced lookers, but our locating average dropped way down. We checked the ministry, the customs office, even nearby coffee houses. But no Sarfraz. He had simply evaporated and nobody would offer a clue.

Five o'clock came and went. The airline cargo office closed.

132

And fifteen minutes later Sarfraz surfaced. He appeared at the hotel while we were still out searching the streets for him, talked to our cameraman, promised to clear the film and ship it himself, and made off with the whole package.

"We never should have let that film out of our hands," Welles groaned when he heard the news. "The only sure way is to do the shipping yourself."

"But we couldn't," I offered, trying to mop up the spilt milk. "The cargo office is closed. And anyway, I'm sure we can trust Sarfraz."

Welles' silence was eloquent.

"I'll check the airline," he said, reaching for the phone, "to make sure that the damn thing is booked on the flight to Karachi. We can have it transshipped from there to New York."

"*Inshallah,*" I added quietly.

The airline had never heard of it; their flight had left with no such parcel aboard. Sarfraz melted away again and we were back in the soup. It was a long sleepless night.

The next day was a tragicomedy of errors.

First thing in the morning Welles blasted Sarfraz out of bed by phone.

"What did you do with my film?" he demanded angrily.

"My dear sir"—Sarfraz yawned—"it is off to New York by now."

"It didn't show on the cargo manifest last night," Welles countered. "Where the hell is it?"

"I didn't trust it to *cargo,*" Sarfraz said soothingly. "A friend carried it by hand. I *told* you that I would take care of it."

"Okay, I'm sorry," Welles said, calming down somewhat. "I will need the flight number and waybill to New York though. Do you have them?"

"Not yet," Sarfraz said. "Let me call you back." But he never did.

At two o'clock we discovered that the film was still in Rawalpindi. I had an apoplectic husband on my hands.

"I'll find that film if I have to tear the cargo office apart!" he said, heading for the door. I raced after him, hoping that Pakistan's jails were coeducational. Baking files inside cakes was not my thing.

Welles had blood in his eye by the time we arrived at the office. I figured that this was no time for calming words, so I kept still. And breathed a sigh of relief when the chief produced a receipt showing that the package had left ten minutes before. And indeed the film arrived in New York, some forty-eight hours late. And worthless! It had not a single image or syllable of sound anywhere on it. The president of Pakistan had been blacked out!

We learned later that Ayub's own men had panicked. They decided privately to prevent the interview from being heard and censored their own president without his knowledge. During the hours the film was missing, it was being exposed to light, all 3,400 feet, and the magnetic soundtrack was wiped clean.

"The irony is," Welles said later, "the bulk eraser they used to blot the whole thing was supplied by American aid. But what they don't know is that I had my tape recorder going the whole time. We have the whole interview right here. Now that all bets are off," he concluded, patting his Uher machine fondly, "I am going to play it to the hilt. We'll just see what happens next."

It usually depresses me when my husband is being expelled from countries. But this was just plain ridiculous. Zulfikar Bhutto blew sky high when he learned that Welles had the tape, and ordered us out forthwith. But before we had time to pack, he had come full circle and invited us back. The erasure story was out by that time and the government wanted it covered up before it reached the president's ear.

Suddenly nothing was too good for the Hangens. Welles was singled out for special interviews, news tips, and favors, which were politely declined.

"We had better get out of here before they give us a camel," Welles said. "Lyndon's friend still has some on hand. And frankly, as the man said when he was ridden out of town on a rail, 'If it weren't for the honor, I'd rather walk.'"

19

On the Beach

Jacqueline Kennedy was expected to take India by storm when she arrived the following week. President John F. Kennedy was dealing with crises elsewhere, so she made the good-will visit on her own. Everything would have been fine except for two small problems: there was no real reason for her trip to begin with, and Mrs. Kennedy seemed to detest the whole thing.

Actually the visit had become something of a fiasco before the fact. It was scheduled, canceled, and rescheduled for months in advance. Then at the last minute it was cut from three weeks to eight days. Resentment spread like ripples all over India.

Cities and entire states which had invested in elaborate preparations were lopped off the itinerary with virtually no notice. Mysore state had spent months rounding up elephants for a lavish parade in honor of the First Lady. It was hard work, especially in springtime when every self-respecting elephant is out in the jungle nuzzling trees. When the visit was summarily canceled, Mysore fumed.

The United States Embassy had its share of problems too although they were largely self-inspired. Mrs. Kennedy's taste in food was one of them.

Press Attaché Clyde Hess was juggling the requests of scores of reporters who had come to cover the story, when his secretary rushed into his office.

"Excuse me, Mr. Hess," she began breathlessly. "It's the grilled cheese sandwiches."

"The what?" Clyde muttered, brushing a hand across his perspiring forehead.

"Mrs. Kennedy's sandwiches," continued the secretary. "A huge box full of bread has just come from Beirut. It has rye bread, whole wheat, French bread, all kinds of bread."

"Bread?" Clyde exclaimed. "Why bread of all things? New Delhi bakes perfectly good bread."

The secretary flushed. "I know, but it goes with the Velveeta cheese we got from Geneva. That came in yesterday, a giant crate of it."

"This place is losing its mind!" exploded the press attaché.

"I know, sir," agreed the girl. "The chef is having a dry-run on sandwich grilling right now. What do you think we should do?"

Clyde groaned. "Obviously there is only one thing *to* do," he snapped in exasperation: "Eat!" And the whole embassy had grilled cheese sandwiches for lunch that day.

Even the lavish dinner held in Mrs. Kennedy's honor was rehearsed in advance, complete with flowers, wines, and stand-in guests. The American Embassy had gone utterly mad.

The nervousness ended when Jackie arrived. Tension gave way to boredom. Formal luncheons and dinners, visits to hospitals and schools, now and then a museum, and she spoke not a word. Except for her frequent changes of stunning clothes, the First Lady's visit was stultifying.

Behind the scenes, however, where television cameras could not peep, there was a very lively periphery. Lee Radziwill was her sister's companion on the visit, and when the day's formal functions were completed the merriment began. Maharajahs outdid each other in dreaming up exotic entertainment for the famous sisters, and some journalists gave up looking for serious issues and simply joined in the fun. While those stories might have made dazzling reading, they were never written.

Other reporters took the dullness as a challenge to their ingenuity and ferreted out side stories to weave into the plot. Welles was among the ferrets, as was NBC's Barbara Walters, whose high professional standards Welles had great respect for. This was one of her first overseas assignments for the "Today" show, and even though the visit had deteriorated into a long-drawn-out fashion show ("What is she wearing? A floating *what?* Double floating panels, you say? Well what color *is* cerise? Couldn't I just say red?"), Barbara Walters refused to leave it at that. Instead she used Jackie's frequent change of costume as a peg for doing a special report on Indian fabrics and saris.

All the reporters tagged along when the party went on to Pakistan. I have never heard my husband grumble so much, but off he went. An assignment is an assignment and you can't win them all. And it was then that I awoke one morning with a temperature of 104 degrees. Fever, chills, delirium: I ached everywhere. The doctor said, "Dengue fever." I thought Kipling has made that one up, but this surpassed even *his* imagination.

My whole world was heat, suffocating, nauseating heat. In fevered fantasy I became a farmer flogging bullocks under scorching Indian suns; a naked Hindustani hunched at searing roadside, comatose, alone; a scrawny Brahma bull, hipbones protruding in sharp ridges, mouth parched, dying of thirst.

"Welles, where are you?" I moaned, thrashing in delirium. "All you care about is your damn story . . . what about *me?* . . . take me out of this awful place, away from those marigolds, ugly marigolds, *Christmas* marigolds . . . don't touch them! . . . they'll burn you too . . ."

The high fever subsided after a few days, but I was still engulfed in a wave of depression.

"Don't worry," the doctor said. "Depression is a normal side-effect of hepatitis. You have a touch of that now, too."

As a diagnostician, he might have been great, but he certainly flunked out in psychology. Don't worry? I was sure that I was dying.

Just before I sent out for the calla lilies, Welles returned from Pakistan. I couldn't meet his plane as I usually did, so I sent a note of explanation with Robert who went instead. Welles' exasperation over the non-story he had been covering, coupled with word of my illness, proved to be too much. Frantic to clear customs and get home, he shoved his cameras onto the counter. They were the same ones he had taken out with him, as his receipt showed. But the inspector chose that moment to argue. With icy calm Welles said, "Cameras? What cameras? Oh no, these aren't *my* cameras. I have just given them to *you*. Take them. They are all yours!" And he wheeled and stalked out of the customs shed.

"Oh please, sir," called the appalled inspector, rushing after him. "They *are* your cameras."

"Don't talk to me about cameras," growled Welles ominously. "I have made *you* a *present*."

NBC stood to lose some valuable equipment right then, except for the fortunate intervention of a friend: the airport director. He sized up the situation, threw his weight at customs, and had the cameras loaded up and put in Welles' car without further protest.

It was right about then that we decided to leave India. My illness and the world's longest fashion show, juxtaposed, were the final straw for Welles. And we both felt that a European assignment was needed, and deserved, after so many years in the Middle East and Asia.

Welles telephoned New York to propose a transfer, and NBC agreed.

"There's just one thing, though, Welles," the news director said into his New York phone. "Before you leave India, we would like to have you go to the Congo. Seems to be something kicking up down there. Just check it out, okay?"

"This is a terrible connection," Welles said. "Sorry, I didn't quite hear what you said. It sounded like you said 'the Congo.' "

"That is exactly what I *did* say," shouted the voice through static. "Just take a week or so and see what's going on. And then, how would you like to make your next assignment Germany?"

"Germany? Great!" my husband said, giving me a wink across the room.

I rushed to his side, smiling broadly. I hugged him, then hugged myself and started dancing happily around the room. We would live in Germany! Castles, symphonies, opera! Wiener Schnitzel, wine! *Real* Christmas, with fir trees instead of marigolds! I could practically smell, taste, and *feel* them all.

138

Then Welles hung up the phone.

"It is great news, sweetheart," he said, catching me in mid-pirouette. "But they want me to go down to the Congo first for a little while—"

"The Congo?" I interrupted, stunned. "Why on earth should you go there? It isn't anywhere near here. *This* is your assignment, not Africa!"

Welles shrugged. "I guess New York is confused by talk of an Afro-Asian world." He grinned. "Probably think it is all one continent."

"Welles, this is ridiculous," I said. "You can't *get* there from here without flying to Europe first. Let them send someone from New York. It would be a lot simpler."

"They probably would if they had someone," Welles countered. "But I do know something about Africa, and that is what they need."

"Oh honey," I pressed, "please call them back and say that you won't go. It makes no sense."

Welles drew a finger across my forehead to erase the frown. "You know better than that," he said gently. "We will take care of this one first, and then we'll move to Germany. This Congo thing shouldn't take long, and you will need packing time anyway. Let's think in terms of two or three weeks, and then we'll head for Bonn."

He left the next morning for the Congo. Neither of us dreamed that it would be five long, lonely months before we could be together again.

I did start to pack for our move to Germany but soon gave it up. It seemed that everything I stowed in the bottom of a trunk turned out to be the very thing I needed most the next day. And as the days went slowly by, I became less and less interested in doing anything at all.

This winter of 1960–61 was definitely for Welles and me the season of our discontent. Shared, in varying degree, by thousands of troubled Africans whose continent was rent by struggles for independence from colonial rule.

The Congo was a prime disaster area. Belgium gave the diverse republic its independence on June thirtieth, but unfortunately gave it little else. The fledgling Congolese leaders had no political training before leaving the nest, and they all wanted to be chiefs, not indians. Kasavubu, Lumumba, Ileo, Adoula, Mobutu, Gizenga, Kalonji, Tshombe: passionate, power-hungry, and hopelessly naive. Tribal warfare erupted, the army mutined against its Belgian officers, and whole provinces began to secede from the newly formed republic. In desperation the government in Leopoldville appealed to the United Nations for a peace-keeping force to hold the country together. In the course of time that force found it had its hands full just trying to keep the new Congo leaders from murdering each other.

Dag Hammarskjöld, then secretary general of the UN, tried personally to mediate among the warring tribal chiefs and was killed in a plane crash near the Congo border almost on the eve of success. Finally United Nations troops were ordered to fight, and within hours an uneasy peace came to the Congo.

Welles was in Leopoldville watching these gyrations. He felt that the inmates of a kindergarten had taken over the world. Nothing made sense except in emotional terms, and everyone had a gun. Neither UN soldier nor Belgian nor newsman was immune from sniper bullet or mob attack.

"Here we lunge from one insanity to another," one letter said, "from one government-that-isn't-a-government to another of the same sort. All signals are reversed here. It makes Lebanon in the summer of 1958 seem like a sober gathering of the American Bankers Association."

With every paroxysm, political or military, the entire Congolese communications system fell apart. Cable and telephone offices closed their doors, air traffic stopped completely, and radio transmission jammed. For those trapped in the Congo the rest of the world ceased to exist.

For a newsman, a story is no story at all if it isn't reported. So a cut telephone line or closed cable office simply means: find another way. Across the Congo River from Leopoldville was Brazzaville, the sleepy capital of a republic formerly governed by the French. Brazzaville was another way, if one could get there.

Welles tried that route one night after an army coup had severed communications totally. He wrote me:

We chartered an outboard motorboat to cross the Congo River because the ferries have stopped running. It was a weird, fantastic trip. Our pilot, a Belgian, had lots of trouble making a proper landfall on the Brazzaville side because of the complete absence of illumination in that down-at-the-heels little French colonial town. Moreover, our boat's propeller kept getting fouled in the huge water hyacinths that float down the Congo. The pilot cautioned us to watch for crocodiles which can be a menace, but it was too dark to see anything so we just listened instead. It was eerie but we made it. I got through to New York from the Brazzaville radio studio at 3:00 in the morning, our time. Then came the trip back across the river, equally wild. But we were home in our hotel by 5 o'clock. An interesting enterprise. . . .

I must sign off now because my courier is about to leave. With no mail service, it is the only way to get letters out. Don't worry about anything. Here there is no danger whatsoever, especially since the trigger-happy Congo army has been put under wraps by the UN. But Henry Taylor, our young Scripps-Howard friend, was killed by a sniper's bullet in the provinces. That was horrible. He was only 30. What a way to die.

Reading his words as I sat alone in our New Delhi home, I found it impossible *not* to worry. Henry Taylor was a good friend of Welles'. He was bright, enthusiastic, happy. Yet he died in mid-career while covering a story. Don't worry about anything? How on earth could I not?

At that moment I decided to go to the Congo too.

One big problem about the news business is that one never can make a firm plan. This Congo story was a perfect example: Welles had expected to be gone only two or three weeks, and it was now almost five months. If I were to fly down to join him now, it was perfectly possible that he would pass me, flying *back*. The cost of an airplane ticket to the Congo from New Delhi would pay our grocery bills for months, and maybe it would all be wasted. My mind was in turmoil. It would be foolish

141

to go, but I could no longer stay here. And the dilemma was compounded by our inability to communicate directly. Phones were out, cables erratic, and letters could get through only when carried by hand. Two of my letters to Welles had been returned when he left Leopoldville for the provinces. The effect was shattering.

The Indian Army had a contingent with the United Nations forces in the Congo then, and the United States Air Force supplied shuttle service. Why not hitch a ride to the Congo with them? It would be free, direct, the fastest possible way to reach my husband.

"And very uncomfortable," said Captain Singh as we discussed the idea in his office that afternoon. "The planes aren't fitted out for passengers, you know. Just bucket seats and they are hard. It gets plenty cold at times, and it's a long trip. No, you really shouldn't try."

"But I can wear fatigues," I argued, "and bring my own food. I honestly wouldn't mind the discomfort. I just want to *get* there. Please?"

Captain Singh examined my press credentials and thought that he might be able to request space on the basis of my being a journalist.

"I can't give the permission myself," he said, "and I'm not sure that I would anyway. It is a darned tough trip." He looked at me curiously and shook his head. "Well, I'll put through your request. But the decision will rest with the U.S. Air Force."

Captain Singh obviously thought I was out of my mind. During the days that followed, many of our friends did too. For the request went not only to the air attaché at the American Embassy, but eventually was kicked all the way upstairs. It came to rest at last in the Washington D.C. office of the United States Joint Chiefs of Staff! We never have known what answer was planned, for Welles returned from the Congo at that juncture.

We were both bone weary. He needed peace and quiet after the interminable rigors of the Congo, but I found it hard to leave him alone. He required room to rally his strength, air to refresh his thoughts. His was the honest exhaustion of overworking and over-thinking. Mine, the mindless fatigue of self-absorption. We had been longing for each other but now that we were together again, each felt a strangeness. We spent those first days almost on tiptoe, approaching each other gingerly. I soon gave up asking questions about the Congo. His answers were vacuous at best, and I began to feel intrusive. At times even resentful. He seemed to want to block out all memory of it, or at least to keep it from me. He countered with questions about friends I had seen and parties I had attended, in a manner so desultory that I stopped answering. Even when we touched we were strangers.

I had been lonely and frustrated while he was away, but that was nothing compared to this. I could *see* the man I loved but he was not there, not for me, at all. He would even start with surprise when I entered a room and get up, quite formally, to greet me. He all but shook my hand.

Suddenly I couldn't stand it any longer. All he did was read, just read. Always sitting there quietly with some damn book or other in his hand, giving it the full and constant attention I never got.

I needed to shock him, to hurt him as he was hurting me. Anything to get through to him. His apathy about himself, about life, about *me,* was more than I could bear. Damn it, *look* at me! At least look at me!

"Welles," I began, aware that my heart was pounding wildly, "do you remember that dinner party I told you about? George brought me home, did I tell you? I invited him in for a while."

Welles went right on reading.

"George stayed, Welles. He stayed a long time. We had some drinks. I was horribly lonely."

He turned a page.

"He stayed all night, Welles. George stayed all night with me, do you hear me? All *night.*" I was out of control now, pacing the room in furious frustration. "My God, don't you care about *anything* anymore?"

He didn't even look up.

"Oh God," I said in desperation, "I can't do it any longer. I

143

can't *live* this way. It wasn't true, what I just said. But don't you see: it *could* be true. Don't you *see? Don't you see?"* I turned away and stared out the window, at nothing.

Then I heard the door open and quietly close. And I heard the sound of Welles' footsteps slowly fading into the night.

We were silent at breakfast the next morning. Each eating slowly, looking only at our plates, saying nothing. We had slept restlessly, pretending sleep, unconsciously avoiding one another. Or perhaps consciously, I wasn't sure which. Sleeping together, worlds apart.

"Welles, what is it?" I asked, breaking the morning's silence, almost too tired to care anymore. "Where *are* you, honey? It's as though you never came back from the Congo. I just can't find you anymore.

"I didn't mean those things I said last night," I went on wearily. "I could never sleep with anyone else, you know that. I wanted to hurt you, to wake you up. But you aren't even *here.*"

To my horror, his shoulders began to shake, his hands dropped to his lap, and his face contorted in agony. Deep sobs shook his whole body. "I don't know," he moaned, "I don't know . . . I don't . . . know."

I jumped up and ran to him. I sank to my knees beside him and took him into my arms.

"Darling, darling, darling . . . it's all right," I said, holding him close. "It's going to be all right. We can do it. We'll get through this, this whatever it is." I was crying now too, holding my husband, holding, holding, breathing words into his ear. "It *will* be all right. We can *do* it."

I don't know how long we stayed that way, sobbing together, holding each other, freeing our torments. But it ended in a quiet exhaustion of spent emotion through which, and beyond which, we held one another ever more closely.

20

The Twilight Zone

When a mind is disoriented it cannot select its own course. That is where love comes in. During those days before we left India we found it possible to share everything, even our most senseless fears. And in so doing, we came to realize that neither of us would ever again be completely alone.

We sailed from India to Europe. Everything was perfect. We had never been so close. Our ship was a small Italian steamer loaded with canneloni and chianti, which added up to heaven for our curried palates. It also had a captain with a dog, which meant that our new Tibetan terrier puppy had the run of the ship with his high-ranking playmate, and could even sleep in our cabin. It was a peaceful journey, unencumbered by pressure or time. We arrived in Naples completely renewed and took the train to Bonn.

German trains are meticulously punctual. They accomplish this by never ever remaining longer than one minute in any station. It is sometimes hazardous for passengers trying to get on and off, but rules are rules. This day not only were we ourselves, trying to get off but we had twenty-three pieces of hand baggage and a dog. Clearly this called for a plan.

Ten minutes before we were due to arrive in Bonn, we began stacking our bags in the entryway. The area measured about twelve feet by eight, but by the time our gear was positioned, it had so shrunk that other passengers had to exhale to get through. Welles suggested that we pile the bags on a teeter balance toward the door. If all else failed, they might fall out of their own weight when the train stopped in the station. But the basic strategy was that I would be the pusher and he the thrower when the door opened. As the train pulled into Bonn station, we were ready to let fly.

The train braked abruptly. We almost hit the floor. The door snapped open and we had a glimpse of a pretty lady on the platform who was smiling broadly in welcome and holding a bouquet of flowers. But it was only a glimpse because she was suddenly obscured by the hail of our baggage being pelted off the train. I pushed, Welles tossed, the bags scattered, the lady ducked. In exactly forty seconds the Hangens were off the train. The pretty lady looked aghast. Welles grinned, a bit embarrassed. The train stood calmly in the station, its door wide open, with twenty seconds still to go. I have never felt quite so foolish.

"You must be Mr. Hangen," said the lady after she had recovered her bouquet from underneath a bag. She introduced herself as Welles' new Bonn assistant, and the expression on her face made it plain that she foresaw a frenetic time ahead.

But by the time our luggage was stashed in her Volkswagen, which was a neat trick in itself, we were laughing and chatting like old friends. We had arrived, if somewhat unceremoniously, in Bonn.

It was well that we arrived when we did. President John F. Kennedy was due in Germany the following week, and Welles found many colleagues in town preparing for what was to be a historic visit. John Chancellor and Ray Scherer were there, both good NBC friends whom he had not seen since we left for India. The three split up assignments, devised systems for circumventing the throng, and were eager for the drama to begin.

President Kennedy's visit coincided with a new East-West confrontation in Berlin. For the first time in nearly two years East German Communists publicly denied Allied military vehicles the right to move freely into East Berlin. They also made sure that East Berliners would not be able to see the President when he visited the Berlin Wall. Thirty-six hours before Kennedy's arrival, the East Germans created a no-man's-land along their side of the concrete and barbed-wire wall that divides the city.

146

Anyone entering that area, even to wave to a friend on the other side, was liable to two years in jail. Photography was banned and heavy penalties were prescribed for anyone damaging the wall or the watchtowers and pillboxes used by East German border guards.

Despite these tensions, Kennedy's welcome in West Berlin was the most tumultuous that the city, and the man it honored, had ever known. At least half a million chanting, cheering, waving West Berliners turned out to see him.

"I don't come here to reassure the people of Berlin," he said when he arrived. "This city reassures *us.*" Then he began his triumphal progress through the city, standing up in the rear of an open convertible with then-Chancellor Konrad Adenauer and West Berlin Mayor Willy Brandt.

Welles had his tape recorder on, doing a running narration of events as they played:

Now President Kennedy is having his first view of the Berlin Wall. We are at Checkpoint Charlie, the main point for foreigners to cross into East Berlin. A platform is erected here on this side of the wall so that the President can look over into the twilight zone beyond. He is standing somberly on the platform now, looking across at the series of concrete walls built to stop the outflow of refugees from East Berlin. The President is looking into the East. Border guards are looking back, through binoculars. President Kennedy seems visibly moved. He is staring at the grim barrier moodily, now walking slowly away. On the other side of the wall there is only silence.

As the President's party moved on, Kennedy caught the crowd's fighting mood perfectly. "Anybody who thinks Communism is the wave of the future should come to Berlin," he roared. "Freedom is not perfect, but we never had to put a wall up to prevent our people from leaving!"

The cheers were thunderous. His brief speech was interrupted frequently by frenzied applause and rhythmic chants of "Kennedy! Kennedy!"

Then, for the first time, the president spoke in German.

"Ich bin ein Berliner!" he shouted over and over again. The packed throng went wild and surged forward, and at that mo-

ment, the Berlin freedom bell tolled somberly over the crowd. The ardor of the Berliners' welcome for John F. Kennedy was exceeded only by their anguish at his death. On the evening of November 22, 1963, thousands of West Berlin students staged a spontaneous torchlight parade to express their grief. Candles were lit in token of mourning in almost every West Berlin window, and in many windows on the other side of the wall as well.

"We felt it even more than you Americans," was one Berliner's epitaph. "He epitomized our hope."

We were back in our Bonn home during that five-month interim between Kennedy's visit and his death. We had a two-bedroom bungalow near the Rhine which Welles' assistant had rented for us before we arrived. Our New Delhi furniture fit in perfectly, and the only things we needed to buy were for the garden and patio behind. We ate most of our meals there, weather permitting, and it was there Welles did much of his writing. After years of hiding like moles from the searing sun, it was wonderful to be able to live outdoors again. One of the nicest things about that garden was watching it change with the seasons. We saw white ermines racing across the snow in winter, and we watched for the first crocus to break through in spring. We had been so starved for seasons that it was downright exciting.

We had hungered too for concerts, opera, and theater, and we got as much of them as we could, but our long walks in the forested hills above the Rhine or along its banks were best of all. Our Tibetan terrier, Igloo, always went along. He was usually well ahead chasing squirrels, or well behind digging after gophers, and one evening along the Rhine he left us altogether to play with some children instead.

"Looks like old Iglettes needs a playmate of his own," Welles said, slipping an arm around my waist.

"Oh, I don't know, honey," I answered. "I think that one dog is enough."

"I wasn't thinking of another dog"—he laughed; "I would like

148

to adopt a child. Have you ever thought about it?"

Thought about it? Yes, I had thought about it a lot. Ever since that devastating experience with Holy Mary Hospital in India. But that was a long time ago. There was no point in reliving it. Besides, Welles was waiting for an answer.

"Yes, I would like to adopt a child," I said. "A newborn to raise as our own. I would really love that."

"You're sure?" he asked, stopping, turning me toward him. "Or would you like to think about it for a while?"

"I *have* thought about it"—I smiled—"for a long time. I have just been waiting for *you.*"

"There are a couple of things we'd better talk about, though," he continued. "For one, we probably won't be able to travel together as much as we have. Will you mind that?"

I thought a moment and then said, "Yes, I probably will because I love covering stories with you. But I really want a family too. Other press wives manage it, so I'm sure I can. But there's one thing I could never do: live back in the States and leave you out here, as some of them do. They think it's safer for the children that way, but to me, living apart wouldn't be *living* at all."

Welles' arm tightened around my waist and he smiled. "I think we'd be great parents," he said thoughtfully, "but our life isn't exactly normal. Is it fair to bring a child into a crazy life like ours?"

"A child needs love, honey," I said. "I don't think there is a home with more love in it anywhere in the whole world. And joy. And dedication. What more does a child *really* need?"

"Well, I'll tell you what," Welles said as we walked on slowly. "We'll find someone good to help you . . . a 'nanny' . . . is that the word? Because I don't ever want you to feel tied down. And then we can have the best of both worlds. What do you say?"

"Wonderful! Absolutely perfect!" I said. "But . . . I haven't the vaguest idea how we go about it, have you?"

"Well, I just happen to have a few things here for us to look at," Welles said, smiling. He took an envelope from his pocket and pulled out a letter. It was from The Cradle, an adoption

149

society in Evanston, Illinois. And it contained an application form.

"Welles Hangen," I said, shaking my head, "you really are too much. I have been hoping you would come round to this idea. But here you are, *way* ahead of me as usual. Bless you. I *do* love you."

"I know you do, baby," he said. "Now, would you rather have a boy or a girl?"

"I honestly don't care which comes first," I said. "But I would like both sometime."

"Good," he said. "So would I. Let's go home and fill out the application right now. They say it'll be a long wait, so let's get started." And he whistled for Igloo, and we turned and raced each other back to the car.

We sent in the forms that day and made plans to visit The Cradle on our next homeleave. But we knew that it would be more than a year before our dream would actually come true.

Meanwhile, our delightful German neighbor and my best friend, Frau Ingeborg Simon, had a girl aged seven and a three-year-old boy, and we spent most of our time together while our husbands were at work. They were good friends too. Dr. Simon had held several important positions in the German government and introduced Welles to his colleagues. Thanks to them, our circle of German friends grew rapidly and we both soon felt at home. While I learned to bake gingerbread men and make mobiles for the Simon children, Welles was exploring German politics. His German was fluent and he was finding his assignment both stimulating and pleasant. So it was with no little annoyance that he greeted a cable from New York one evening.

We had just returned from another walk along the Rhine and were looking forward to a quiet dinner at home when the telephone rang. Welles answered it in the adjoining room and I heard him taking down the cable, repeating each word as it came.

When I heard "Cyprus" and "soonest," I ran to the kitchen and turned all fires up to high. If he planned to take off for that troubled island tonight, it certainly would not be on an empty stomach.

150

Then he called the airlines. There were no flights out until the next morning. I turned the fires off again, and made us each a drink instead.

"I don't like the sound of this," Welles said when he came back into the room. "The earmarks are all too familiar."

"You mean Lebanon all over again?" I asked.

"Yes, in a different setting," he said thoughtfully. "Greece and Turkey. Egypt and Israel. India and Pakistan. I guess you have to know someone really well to hate him." He took a sip of his drink, straightened, and said, "Well, *plus ça change, plus c'est la même chose*. I only wish that we could break the pattern somehow."

Welles was scheduled out on an eight o'clock flight the next morning, so we were both up in time to hear the six o'clock news. He was taking a bath and I was sliding eggs into a pan for sunnyside-up when the newscaster said: "Two NBC correspondents were shot on Cyprus today."

My God, I thought. That's all we need. *Now* they're shooting the *press!*

Then I raced upstairs to tell Welles. We stared at each other for a moment, shocked speechless.

"Well, let's get moving," he said hoarsely. "I guess they'll need me more than ever now."

When there is nothing to say, it is best not to say anything. But you can certainly *feel* a lot. I rode along with him to the airport that morning with a chunk of granite lodged on the back of my neck. My nerves were tied up in knots and I felt the same apprehension I had felt that day, so long ago, when we drove to the Syrian border from Beirut. Certain that disaster lay ahead, yet equally certain that there was nothing I could do about it. I held Welles' hand tightly and prayed that once again we would make it through.

There was no further news before the plane took off. It was the hardest goodbye I had ever said, and I returned home sick with apprehension. Had the correspondents been shot *because* they were reporting? Or was it another inexplicable accident of war? At that moment we did not know.

Later that day word came that it had in fact been an accident. The correspondents' car had hit a road mine, and although one was seriously injured they had both survived. Feeling grateful to God that it had not been worse, I settled back to wait for a letter. It wasn't long before one came.

All is confusion here. [Welles wrote] Almost a carbon copy of Lebanon in 1958. I should have brought along my old scripts. Changing a few proper names would bring everything perfectly up to date. Even the mouldering roadblocks look the same. It is painfully familiar, down to the atrocity charges that fall freely from the lips of Turks and Greeks alike. The Cypriots are extremely attractive. I like both Greeks and Turks on this island. It is grotesque that they should be killing one another.

According to Welles, NBC had a "cast of thousands" there and he had been put in charge.

"That has an ominous ring of permanency about it," he wrote. "But I'm hopeful that I can get out next week."

Having learned the hard way about the vagaries of such assignments, I knew that it was time for me to find something intriguing to do on my own.

In the dense, dark Franconia forest bordering East Germany stands a thousand-year-old castle called Lauenstein. Its turrets, ramparts, arched gateway, and moat are out of a fairytale, and its height commands the whole area. There, suns set behind forests and mountains, and night fogs come slowly down the ravines and float up to cover each tree and peak in turn.

But all the beautiful wooded slopes and valleys above Lauenstein are silently empty: they are in East Germany. A strip, thirty yards across, belts all hills and fields with barbed-wire fences and mines. Timber was cleared in many places to create this monstrous girdle, and throughout the forest small roads bump into it and suddenly cease to be.

I drove the area one day, trying every side road into the forests. Each wound through a tiny village and then led off to another, which it never reached: barbed wire cut it abruptly and the rest was overgrown with weeds, completely erased.

One dirt road that I followed went through a town called Tettau and wanted to go on to Spechtsbrunn, two kilometers away. It climbed through cedar woods so dense no light could penetrate. But the top of the hill was empty of trees, and the usual barbed wire cut the road.

Getting out to inspect the fence, I found a crude map attached to a post. It warned of five further fences beyond and pinpointed the mined strip. Growing behind were masses of purple wildflowers which stretched through the barbed wire as if they too wanted out. And a solid carpet of purple sage covered the mines.

When I left the dismal place, I could feel spyglasses trained on my little red Volkswagen as it bumped up and down those chopped-off roads, stopping and retreating at each barbed-wire block. But I hoped that my timing might be good enough to give some escaping East German a ride to town.

Chilled to the bone, I stopped at a cafe in Ludwigsstadt for a warming cup of coffee. There I learned that just the day before three men had escaped through that same barbed wire.

"It seems an awful gamble to me," I said, "with that mined area and five barbed-wire fences."

But the waiter replied, "It is death either way. They want freedom enough to risk it."

Later as I sat in my room in Lauenstein Castle, which now lodges travelers, I looked into the east. Evening fogs swirled down the ravines and smoothed the forests. Shadowy figures seemed to be creeping toward me, hiding under those silent mists.

"May God help you," I said quietly. "Please make it!"

Sleep came very slowly that night. In the morning I drove swiftly away, but the chill went with me. Music would help dispel it, I thought, so I decided on the Wagner Festival in Bayreuth. Just what I needed, if I could only get there. But the Germans don't make it easy.

Lufthansa did not fly to Bayreuth in those days. But they did go to Frankfurt, which was halfway, and something called Air Lloyd went on to the festival city. So I headed for Frankfurt.

153

At the airport I searched for the Air Lloyd counter but couldn't find it.

"Oh yes," said the smiling lady in the information booth. "I'll phone them for you."

Twenty minutes went by. I went back to the desk, thinking that she had misunderstood, and inquired again.

"Yes," she said, her smile becoming a giggle, "he will be right over to get you."

Soon a stocky little man loped through the door and up to the counter, announcing brightly: "Air Lloyd!" I waved and he came over, picked up my bag, and told me to follow him.

We walked all the way around the terminal, past both the arrival *and* departure buildings, and came finally to an open runway where there was a little tiny shack with the words AIR LLOYD painted over the door. Standing in front of the shack was a little tiny airplane which also said AIR LLOYD. It was the kind with a propeller on its nose and small stubby wings. I began to fret.

The man beckoned me into the office. He sold me a ticket, put my money in his pocket, picked up my bag, and took me out to the baby plane. Then he stowed my bag, hopped into the pilot's seat, and started the motor. This was clearly Lloyd himself: a one-man airline!

The passenger cabin was right behind the pilot's seat without benefit of partition. It was fitted out for four people, if they knew each other well, with seat straps for each. And the windows came straight down to the floor, so visibility was great.

It turned out that we had just one passenger that day: me. So we took off ahead of schedule. Quite a crowd collected to watch our departure, which was not surprising: I had never seen anything quite like it either. And I waved rather bleakly to all as we revved up our little prop and taxied bumpily off toward the big boys' runway.

Actually it was kind of fun. The air wasn't rough and I floated through the skies thumbing slowly through my *Tannhäuser* libretto in solitary splendor. The only tiny nagging thought that I kept pushing out of my mind was: What if something happens to *him?*

But Lloyd and I made it to Bayreuth without mishap. As we landed, he looked back at the gray skies and said, "We're lucky to have such good weather. Yesterday I brought a lady here, and when she got out of the plane she lost a shoe in the mud." The airport was a vacant lot with patches of purple thistles. Air Lloyd obviously had a clear monopoly.

But the festival was glorious. The town ate, drank and breathed Wagner. The trouble was that when the music stopped, the silence of the eastern border returned, bringing with it a depression I could not shake.

"You shouldn't have gone there alone," Welles said when we spoke of my day in Franconia later. We had returned from our journeys and were sharing impressions over dinner, celebrating with candles and wine.

"One wrong turn and you would have been in real trouble," he said earnestly. "Don't do that again, please. It's nothing to fool around with."

I nodded. "I guess you're right," I said quietly. "But the thought of those poor people haunts me. They must be absolutely miserable to take such chances."

"They obviously are," Welles replied thoughtfully, "but I'm wondering about the others, the ones who stay behind. Why don't we go into East Germany and find out instead of guessing. Would you like that?"

Welles began making plans for our first trip behind the Iron Curtain, but he had another Kennedy assignment to handle first. This time it was Robert Kennedy, on his way through to Poland. It was sure to be a good story, but there was just one little problem: Welles didn't have a Polish visa.

"We can't take you along without a visa," said Kennedy's press secretary on the telephone that night. "And anyway, our embassy in Warsaw says that the government will not allow any extra people. We have twenty in the party already."

"Are there any newsmen on the plane?" Welles asked, knowing full well that there weren't. But it was as good an opening shot as any.

With the negative reply, he drove the point further. "Surely Mr. Kennedy would like press coverage of his historic trip. I'm

155

willing to take my chances with the Polish government."

There followed much hemming and hawing and promises to call back.

This went on for most of the night. And finally about four-thirty A.M., the weary press secretary gave qualified agreement to the plan. Welles could go along on the plane as far as Frankfurt, their take-off point to Poland, and they would see what happened then. We went happily off to bed for a brief night's sleep.

My baggy-eyed husband left the next morning, highly excited. He had never been to Poland and was determined that this gamble should work.

"You go on back to Bonn, honey," he said with a kiss. "If I get bumped in Frankfurt I'll meet you at home. If I make it, well, we'll play that one by ear." Since we play life that way anyway, I was pretty sure of what would happen.

Sure enough, a Frankfurt newsman phoned me in Bonn that afternoon to report that Welles had made it: He was on his way to Poland. I wondered what Warsaw officials would think when the party of twenty was now twenty-one. But . . . Polish prisons and arbitrary injustice were best forgotten. After all, I told myself again and again, he was safe with Kennedy.

As it turned out, Robert Kennedy was delighted by Welles' tenacity and he slipped the one unvisaed passport in among those that had been properly stamped. When the plane landed in Warsaw, the batch was given over to Polish customs in one stack. Kennedy told Welles to stay with him, and the two men left in an embassy car before the passports were even checked.

American Embassy officials were left spinning like dervishes. This simply was not done. Entering any country without a visa is dicey, but . . . Poland?

Robert Kennedy simply left instructions for the embassy to take care of it. But talking a hostile government into giving a visa under such circumstances would be about as easy as getting a bear cub away from its mother, so they assigned Welles an escort officer instead, to keep him from becoming "an incident."

156

By the time airport officials discovered the unvisaed passport, the culprit was in his hotel room busily unpacking his bag.

"You must leave the country on the next plane west!" ordered the Polish policeman sternly when he finally caught up.

But the next plane west belonged to a Polish national airline which refused to accept Welles' credit card. For once my husband did not argue.

"The government of Poland *orders* you to leave," said the officer even more sternly.

"I can't," Welles said happily. "Your national airline won't take me, so I will just have to wait for KLM tomorrow." He shrugged and said innocently, "Sorry, but there is really nothing I can do."

The police officer was trapped and he knew it. Short of taking up a collection for an airplane ticket, he would have to let the felon stay until the capitalist world could carry him out on credit.

"Very well," the Pole growled, "but if you leave the hotel, you will be arrested!" And he left, stationing guards at all the exits on that floor.

Since Welles' room was on the same floor as the Kennedy suite, who wanted to leave anyway? He was included in all of the briefing sessions and had plenty of time to talk with embassy officers who were full of Warsaw news. And that evening he met Robert Kennedy again in the hallway.

"How are you doing?" Kennedy asked warmly. "Come on into my room for a while," he urged. "I would like to talk to you." And they sat up half the night in conversation.

Welles had enough news for three hot-line broadcasts to New York before being ushered out the next day. The Polish government had kept him under guard, but they forgot about the telephone. For one night, that Warsaw hotel room was an NBC broadcasting studio and it probably has never recovered from the shock.

21

Only Life Is Green

If you ever travel to East Germany, be sure to take a dog. If you don't have one, rent one. It is the only way to circumvent state control and see the country plain.

We discovered this quite by accident. Since it was our first visit to the East Zone, and we were not sure how much time we would need, we were loath to board our dog Igloo. So we took him along. We knew that he would more than pay his way in introductions, but the added role he was to play came as a delightful surprise.

The three of us entered East Germany that day at the southwestern border crossing of Wartha, where the German Democratic Republic (DDR) protrudes into West Germany. The border was deserted except for a lone customs shed. On both sides ghost villages hid in dark pine forests. A train track ran alongside the road up to that point, but all signals along it were in the "stop" position. Rails were rusted over and whole segments were missing. Weeds and candytuft pushed up through the ties and all was utterly quiet. Once the crowded Frankfurt-Berlin Express ran the track, but no train had passed this way in years.

Few cars came through either. Welles had to put our Volkswagen in low to deal with the potholes as we approached the shed. A rasp of martial music came from the radio in a window, but all else was still.

The inspector glanced up sullenly from his desk as we entered. But he livened, in the usual manner, at the sight of our dollars and passports. And he even managed a smile when

158

Welles asked to buy hotel vouchers and gas coupons for our trip through the East Zone. This was required by DDR law, ostensibly to make it easier for travelers since they would not have to cope with foreign exchange problems along the way because every single thing had been paid for in advance. In fact, the government was making sure that it got every last cent; our vouchers were valid only in state-controlled concerns. We were being neatly restricted from going elsewhere. Or, at least, that is what they thought.

The inspector stamped our passports, pocketed our dollars, and went out to check the car. The sight of Igloo sitting calmly in the front seat stopped him for a moment. He turned back toward us, hesitated, then shrugged and moved on. Our money felt good in his pocket, and short of boarding a dog in his customs shed indefinitely, there was no solution. Then he poked suspiciously at the Hershey cartons and the crate of oranges stashed in our trunk, frowned, and shrugged again. Clearly he considered us a bit odd, but he didn't want a problem. We glanced at each other with relief. The oranges and chocolates were to be gifts for new friends along the way and we would have hated to lose them here.

Next, using a long rod with mirror attached, he checked underneath the car.

"What on earth is he looking for now?" I whispered to Welles.

"Guns probably. And Western literature. Anything dangerous like that," he said wryly. "But this is nothing compared to what we will get coming out. I'm told that they tear your car apart looking for escaping East Germans: seats out, floorboards raised, trunk walls probed. It will be a complete Beetle physical, Eastern border-guard style. So be happy for now. This is a breeze."

Inspection completed, we started slowly up the winding forest road in search of the autobahn to Weimar. Watchtowers loomed above the trees like creations of a giant erector set, but the mined strip and barbed wire were obscured by foliage. There were no other cars on the road and not a soul in sight.

"Feel those eyes, though," Welles said softly as we crossed a clearing in the forest. "The guards up in their tower are not missing a move we make."

I pulled Igloo onto my lap and tried to cover him with a jacket. We should have taken the extras when we bought this car, I thought. What we need now are blinds!

"Don't worry," he added, noting my discomfort. "They know that we cleared customs or we wouldn't be here. It's the people heading the other way without passports that they are watching for."

I remembered the fogs around my border castle and all the spectres of that night returned. Feeling suddenly gloomy, I asked for the hundredth time, "Why are we always going into places that everyone else is trying to leave?"

"Because, my love," Welles said quietly, "we don't *know* that they *are*."

He was right. Viewed from the other side of the border, East Germany was a huge open-cell prison where seventeen million people dreamed only of escape. A land living under the gun, waiting for a break-out or rebellion. But was it? Escapees clearly felt so, but theirs were the only voices heard. No journalist had been allowed in the East Zone without a communist guide, so the other millions remained silent. Now Welles had permission to wander freely and talk to whomever he wished. With fluent German and a little bit of luck, he might unwind the skein and get at the truth.

The forest road turned onto an autobahn then and we were startled to find it deserted. A child could have played jacks on the white center line, and the lack of oil spills told us that it was always like this. We did meet a few cars as we neared Weimar but they all looked handmade: disparate parts assembled, with Mercedes-Benz stars rigged like prow figures in front. Their passengers ogled our plain little VW as though it were a mini-limousine, and it suddenly seemed to prance along the road.

Then we crossed the Ilm River and had our first glimpse of Weimar. The quiet cobbled streets wound past graying rococo townhouses with sagging slate roofs and eighteenth-century court residences of peeling ochre and red.

"It is still beautiful," Welles said as he swung into another

160

silent street, "but think how it must have looked in Goethe's day. It was one of the cultural centers of the world then, humming with life."

"Does anyone remember?" I asked. "Everything is peeling and turning gray. They aren't taking care of it at all, just letting it die."

"With dignity, at least," Welles replied. "The bulldozers never got this far. They've smashed the beauty out of other cities. Actually Weimar is lucky."

We were to see piles of rubble which had once been palaces littering the larger East German cities, the war damage indistinguishable from bulldozer destruction. But Weimar had escaped; her classic refinement was left untouched. Even Goethe's house remained a national monument.

But the city's beauty was largely façade, as we discovered on entering the historic Hotel Elephant, made famous by Thomas Mann. The exterior had been left intact, but the Communists had removed its heart. The lobby, once silken and filled with music, was a cavernous waiting room devoid of color. A few Russian soldiers in overstuffed chairs fingered their beer glasses listlessly, but the rest of the hall was empty. The once-glittering dining room was grimy and smelled of cooking fat. Our room had decayed to dinginess and even the bedsheets were torn. Quite obviously nobody cared.

I was dismayed. The Germans, of all people! Nobody loves cleanliness more than they. I wondered what had happened to their spirit.

"No, it's pride that is missing, I think," Welles said. "They have no pride in their work. Everything here is owned by a faceless state, so how can they? I wouldn't want to work for a theory, would you? Unless we believed it ourselves."

"It looks as though few do," I said. "This place is really terrible. Even *I* keep house better than this."

Welles let that one pass. "The thing to do is talk to people *off* the job, where they can't be overheard," he said. "Then I think we'll find lots of spirit. And I expect they will be eager to talk."

He was right. It surprised me at first, since we were foreign-

161

ers. But it soon became clear that foreigners seemed safer confidants than neighbors, and they were desperately eager to talk. This was particularly true in Dresden, but for an unexpected reason.

We arrived there very late one night after driving up from Weimar, and went directly to the Astoria Hotel as our voucher indicated. It was the largest hotel in town and totally unesthetic. But because it was new, the manager plainly considered it the finest in the world and was bound to protect it at all costs.

"You cannot bring that *dog* in here," he said haughtily, glaring at little inoffensive Igloo. "This happens to be a deluxe hotel. No dogs."

Welles handed him our voucher. He read it and looked less certain, for the paper was tantamount to a government order.

Gazing bleakly around his beloved lobby, he looked back at the voucher, then looked at the dog. A battle was raging within. He could not overrule the government, but he loved his antiseptic citadel and could not endure its desecration.

Then abruptly he stood back, straightened his shoulders, and thrust out his jaw. He had made his decision. Bring on the firing squad, and to hell with the blindfold!

"No dogs!" he said firmly, and pushed the voucher back across the desk.

Just as I was about to argue that the Hotel Elephant in Weimar had taken us, Welles gave me a wink, pocketed the paper, and headed for the door. It wasn't like him to give in so easily, and I was confused.

"Don't you see?" he whispered as we left. "Now we can stay anywhere we like. And this time it won't be a place spruced up for Western tourists. What a break!" He picked up Igloo and hugged him as we hurried to the car.

Finding another hotel was not easy, however, and it was now nearly midnight. We drove through Dresden's dark, deserted streets for more than an hour and I was horrified by what we saw: block after vacant block of desolation interspersed with mountains of stone rubble; a block or two of sterile Stalinesque office buildings; more vacancy, more rubble, and an occasional

162

bombed-out cathedral shell looming grotesquely, almost accusingly, in the moonlight.

We had crossed the Elbe by this time and were heading toward the older residential section, away from the desolate inner-city, when suddenly we came to a brightly lighted area, several blocks long, and found people. The first people in groups whom we had yet seen. Some were strolling hand in hand, others were window shopping, and still others were quite boisterously drunk.

"*This* is more like it," Welles said, pulling over to a curb. "Let's see if there is a hotel out here. We will learn more here in two minutes than we could in a week downtown."

A young man approached our car curiously, and Welles put our question to him in German. He offered to direct us to the Park Hotel Weisser Hirsch, a historic place nearby, but he warned that it catered only to guests from Communist countries.

Welles smiled at that. I knew that he was thinking, "So much the better!" If we could get in, we would have a clear shot at a story. Two Americans staying with a bunch of Communists in a celebrated East German hotel whose staff had lodged the elite of Europe in days past. It could be a view of the whole country in microcosm if we were lucky.

The hotel lobby was badly neglected. A few faded travel posters hung forgotten on dingy walls. The acrid smell of cheap cleaning fluid spoiled the air, and the lighting was gloomily dim. But just off the lobby was a restaurant and bar which appeared to be the "in place" for Dresden's middle class. Some were dancing to the music of a Czech band while others crowded together at tables, drinking dark beer or Hungarian wine. Judging from the decibel level, they were having a whale of a time. We couldn't wait to join them.

Fortunately the lady at the reception desk was of the prewar staff, quite willing to bend a rule now and again, so we got a room. Word spread quickly in the bar that we were Americans now living in West Germany, and the crowd welcomed us warmly; and although knots of Russians seated together made

163

a point of ignoring us, as did several East German soldiers who fingered their uniform collars self-consciously, we sat with the others most of the night in deep, cordial discussion.

Before coming to East Germany, Welles had collected letters of introduction to educators, industrialists, writers, students, even Communist Party officials, in order to hear every possible view. Encounters such as these at the Park Hotel were to glue the mosaic together and allow the picture to emerge. Through the surface grayness we began to find spots of vivid color: the farmer's pride in working his own minuscule plot at night, after having given his day to the state; the architect drawing bread-box buildings for pay, and finding solace later in his private blueprints; the artist smuggling his work out to the West, and the writer keeping his concealed. Theirs was a dogged determination to take pride in themselves, at least, and it relieved the tedium.

The oranges and chocolates in our trunk helped us to meet people too, but our supply of the rare goodies dwindled rapidly. Welles gave one of our last oranges to a little girl in a Leipzig park one morning. She was timid at first, and appeared not to know what it was, but curiosity overcame fear, and with her first bite she was all smiles. Welles talked to her mother and learned that Leipzig markets have oranges only at Christmas time, and even then the cost is prohibitive.

"Can that really be true?" I whispered as we wandered on through the park. "If they have oranges just once a year, they probably never find a melon or pineapple ever."

"She said that most good food goes to the Russian troops first," Welles said. "And they are all over the country, as you know."

But on the night we decided to go to the Leipzig opera, I was wholly unprepared for what we saw.

Lights from the opera house glowed along the dim avenue like bright beckoning fingers. Shapes, approaching through darkness, slowly took form as they neared the brilliant citadel. Moving soundlessly like moths clustering to light, they joined the throng inside. It was a capacity crowd, but subdued. The women wore ancient silks and brocades which carried the scent of mothballs, and the men's dark suits were shiny and threadbare. Several young men had outgrown theirs completely, giving a sprinkling of bare wrists and ankles to the scene. The Berlin Wall had severed the flow of imports from the West, and East Germany's producers had no time for finery.

Inside, the contrast between the appearance of the audience and their glorious opera house was as if two worlds were viewing each other, with modern Leipzig losing by default. The walls are of white Meissen porcelain and Swiss pear wood; Italian marble encases the windows, and exquisite crystal chandeliers shed a soft light over all. Even the sets were brilliant that night, and the cast wore splendid new satins and brocades. And the people who could have stayed home, embarrassed by deprivation, sat and looked and listened with pride.

Slowly we began to understand these East Germans. They had been to the mat and had survived, with their sense of values strengthened. After struggling with adversity for over twenty years, alone and unaided, they had come to think of themselves as a people apart. No longer did they view their country as the truncated part of a larger Germany. No longer did they hope to catch up with the West, for they saw the breadth of the discrepancy. What had been a sullen acceptance of fate had become pride in the slightest accomplishment. Envy of the West had slowly changed to bitterness, and their anger at a state which they felt had impeded them was now subtly spreading to their blood brothers across the German border.

"They had it easy," was a phrase we heard repeatedly.

"You gave them everything with your American aid," others said. "Now they drive over here in shiny new cars, flaunting their diamonds and furs."

And an East Berliner summed up what we found to be the general feeling: "Everything we have done, we have done ourselves," he said. "It may not look like much yet. But you will see, in time."

This man spoke not a word about reunification of the two Germanies and, with the exception of the very old, neither did anyone else. Throughout our probing, the words of Mephistopheles rode with us: "All theory is gray," he said to Faust. "Only life is green."

22

Now We Are Three

We lived in Germany until the winter of 1965. During the final months we were in constant contact with The Cradle, waiting for word of our first baby. We had visited there the previous Christmas and had been charmed by all we saw, heard, and felt. And when we met Hazel Ferguson, the director of that gracious estate, we knew that Cradle children would be blessings indeed. All that we needed was a signal from them and we would move back home because we would have to be nearby to allow for periodic staff visits after the baby was ours.

In what proved to be a miracle of timing, Welles was awarded a fellowship from the Council on Foreign Relations in New York for a year's study in the States. We had both become interested in China, having watched her influence increase in India and Asia, and we thought that an assignment in Hong Kong would be an intriguing next step. NBC agreed, so Welles arranged for a leave of absence in order to study Chinese affairs at Columbia University. He would also write his East Germany book *and* become a father.

"What are you going to do with the *rest* of your time?" I asked, amused at our audacity in planning for the year.

"Start learning Mandarin, of course," he answered, laughing too. "What the hell, honey, we have a whole year. We might even take in a Broadway show."

Then The Cradle summoned us home. They had a baby boy for us. We were to come as quickly as possible to see him and decide if he would be ours.

166

Suddenly and inexplicably I panicked.

Maybe having a baby will change us after all, I thought. Maybe it's *not* the right thing to do. We will never be alone again, just the two of us, ever. Maybe we're really better the way we are now.

I tried to tell Welles how I felt, but it didn't come out as I intended.

"Don't you want a baby after all?" he asked. The disappointment in his voice made me cringe.

"Yes, of course I do," I said. "But, I don't know . . . I just . . . oh Welles, darling, I guess I'm just scared to death."

"Hey . . ." Welles began. Then, instead of talking, he held me close in his arms as I tried to understand this bewildering emotion. We had talked of little else for months and I had thought that I was prepared. What on earth was wrong with me now?

"If we had been watching him grow for nine months, I think it would be different," Welles said gently. "But you're an *instant* mother, honey. Of course you're overwhelmed, now that it's happened. I am too. But it's not going to change us, you know that. We'll have someone else to do it all for, and we'll have more fun than ever."

I remembered that day on the Rhine River bank so many months ago, the day when it all began. What we are doing is right, I thought again. When I see the baby, everything will be fine.

I felt calmer then. "I believe that too," I told him. "I guess my nerves are showing is all."

Whoever coined "little stranger" wasn't just whistling Dixie. When we first saw our baby sleeping soundly in his pristine white crib at The Cradle, he looked like a little doll. The trouble began when I picked him up. He opened his eyes, looked up at my face . . . and started to bellow!

"Welles, please, *you* take him," I implored. "He . . . he seems to be afraid of me." The baby was absolutely yowling.

"Take a look at yourself." Welles laughed, reaching for the child. "How can you blame him?"

167

In my self-consciousness over what I had expected would be an intensely poignant moment, I had forgotten the surgical mask covering my face, and my immaculate but shapeless white gown. I was willing to shed them right then. This was a beautiful child and I knew that I would love him dearly. If only he would stop screaming at me!

Welles calmed the baby almost magically, making soothing conversation that I wouldn't have believed. The two seemed to identify immediately. There was no doubt that this would be our son, and that conviction got us through the seemingly interminable court process that followed. The judge spoke in "befits" and "behooves" and even threw in a few "beholdens" for good measure before signing our preliminary adoption papers. But even though his fatuous manner drove Welles straight up the wall, nothing could have lessened our joy.

After court we flew on to New York, carrying our new son, and made our way to the Hotel Des Artistes on Central Park West, our interim home, eager for our first night of parenthood. It turned out to be the night the entire east coast of the United States blacked out.

A power failure in a brand-new home is one thing. But a power failure in a brand-new home with a brand-new baby is something else again. We had no light, no heat, no water, and *no* idea how to take care of a baby. If we put him on his back, he cried; on his stomach, we were sure that he would suffocate. Carrying him around was fine, but the apartment was so small, so unfamiliar, so dark that we kept bumping into things. This woke him up again and the round of putting him down, turning him over, and picking him up started all over again.

"Maybe if we had more candles it would help," Welles suggested, heading for the door. "I'll go buy some."

"Well for heaven's sake, *hurry,*" I said. "He won't stop crying. Do you suppose he's sick?"

"I suppose he is hungry," Welles said impatiently. "If I don't get more candles soon we won't even be able to see him, much less feed him."

"But we can't feed him cold milk," I protested. "The stove is off too."

168

"I'll get the candles," Welles said, more gently now, although he was just as nervous as I. "And I'll try to find a bottle warmer with batteries. Try to relax while I'm gone. And, Pat, please don't drop the baby."

"You're a big help!" I said as the door closed behind him. That was all I needed. I had never felt so awkward and clumsy in my life. I was sure that if I even joggled our son he would break, but . . . drop him? Thanks a lot, Daddy! I'll hang in, but you'd better make it back fast.

Finally Welles returned, not only with candles and a bottle warmer but also with every baby toy in the store, so we made it through the night. The apartment was brighter than a cathedral at Christmas and neither of us slept a wink, but our well-fed, breathing baby did. And in several quarters, little Dana is still known as "the black-out kid."

Those New York months were frantic but immeasurably happy. Dana grew rapidly, and once we learned that babies are made of sponge rubber and do not break, we enjoyed him thoroughly. There were small crises of course, like the time he rolled off our picnic blanket in Central Park and was almost in the lake before we caught him. We forgave those squirts in the eye during diaper changes, and when I began to feel confined because he couldn't be left alone, Welles simply packed him up and he went along with us, so the strain diminished. When we went to classes at Columbia, we went *en famille.* Everything worked so smoothly that when it came time to leave for Hong Kong and we started moving out, it seemed we had only moved in. As we boarded our plane with a baby and a dog, we felt that we were moving the world.

But our majestic white house on Victoria Peak was waiting for us, so the transition was smooth. This was fortunate because our habit of landing smack in the midst of big stories had stayed with us. This time it was the outbreak of China's Cultural Revolution, which was soon to spill over into Hong Kong and lap at the very foot of our peak.

23

Straddling the Fault

China's great Cultural Revolution began as one man's attempt to overthrow a Communist elite which he himself had helped to install in power. It was a coup d'état by Mao Tse-tung against his own regime, an attempt to remove unresponsive officials by mass pressure.

Mao regarded the young postwar generation in China as unworthy to inherit his brand of Communism, and the older generation of leaders as unable to defend it. So he unleashed his young Red Guards on everything old, including old party bureaucrats. He would temper the young and intimidate their elders and produce a new generation of "revolutionary successors."

But to everyone's surprise, the intended victims of Red Guard fury fought back by organizing their own gangs of toughs. Had they not, the revolution might have ended as it began: in an extended parade of human mortification. Instead there was now widespread chaos in the whole of that once tightly disciplined land.

Red Guard fury scorched foreigners as well. More than half the forty foreign embassies in Peking were subjected to abuse. The British mission was an early target.

Journalists were not exempt from irrational passions either, as we learned to our horror when Reuters correspondent Anthony Grey was placed arbitrarily under house arrest. The young British newsman had been in Hong Kong just two weeks before, enroute to his new assignment in Peking. We had dined together that night and found him filled with excitement at the prospect of living in China.

"What happened to Tony?" I asked Welles, stunned at the news. "What on earth did he do?"

"Nothing, absolutely nothing except *be* there," Welles answered grimly. "The Chinese arrested him in reprisal for Communist newsmen jailed here in Hong Kong last week. If the British release these Chinese, Tony will be freed. A very nasty business."

"But the Communist reporters arrested here aren't correspondents from Peking," I protested. "They live here and work for Hong Kong papers. It makes no sense."

"And Tony gets the brunt," Welles finished gloomily. "Two weeks in Peking, and now this. He hardly had time to unpack."

Tony Grey had been on a merry-go-round that day in Hong Kong. He had had too much to do, and no time to do it all. So I did his household shopping. I could hear his voice now as he said, "Don't stint on quality. They may have to last a long time."

Who could have known that those sheets, cases, and towels would have to last and last? For Anthony Grey lived in solitary confinement in Peking for two long, lonely years.

Only scrawny wire fences separated Hong Kong from China's tumult those days. British Gurkha soldiers faced Chinese troops along the wandering little Shumchun River that marked the seventeen-mile boundary. As disorder mounted in China, a massive new barbed-wire barricade known as Snake was hastily built by the British, deeper inside Hong Kong's New Territories. Snake crawled over the mountains and through rice paddies like a miniature and equally useless Maginot Line.

As symbols go, Snake was fine. It lay four hundred yards from the border at its nearest point, giving the British what they called "flexibility to deal with intruders" without risking an armed clash with the Chinese. But everyone in the Colony knew that if a showdown came, the Chinese would be over Snake like a jumprope.

The spillover into Hong Kong was gradual at first. Crude wall

171

posters insulting the British began to appear, and students in a handful of Communist schools were drilled in Red Guard tactics. Oyster farmers were kidnapped by Chinese militiamen who sailed brazenly into Hong Kong waters. Then Red Guards from China demonstrated outside a British police post on the border, but throughout, Hong Kong's government studiously avoided reprisal.

"They are afraid of rocking the boat," Welles explained as we discussed these ominous signs. "One phone call from China would make the British leave. There won't be war over Hong Kong, and these people know it. So the government will do anything to avoid a fight.

"Peking too, I think," he continued. "China makes over six hundred million dollars from here as it is, and who wants to kill a golden goose? Why feed four million more people if England will do it instead? No," he said, "China wants this boat steady too. A little motion now and then, perhaps, but sinking is out."

But when rioting began in Hong Kong itself, we began to wonder. It seemed that the boat was rocking wildly already.

It was May, 1967. The Cultural Revolution was in full storm throughout China. The tiny Portuguese enclave of Macao, just twenty-two miles across the water from Hong Kong, had capitulated to Communist rioters and was under Chinese control although Portuguese officials remained as figureheads. Communists in Hong Kong expected the same tactic to work against the British.

Welles left for the office early that morning. We planned to lunch later at a favorite meeting place hidden inside the imposing cluster of banks in Queen's Road Central.

But then Welles phoned me from town.

"You had better stay home today, honey," he said excitedly. "Queen's Road has gone crazy. Communists marching up and down both sides of the street, waving Mao's little red book. They are swarming around the banks, and a whole wolfpack is mobbing up the hill to the governor's house. It looks mean," he said. "I don't want you in it."

Then: "I'll call you later," he said abruptly. "Here they come!

I want to get film of this!" And he hung up.

From our vantage point in Barker Road on the side of Victoria Peak, it is possible to look directly down into town. I ran outside, binoculars in hand, hoping to see the commotion. To my surprise, the road was blocked bumper-to-bumper with other peak residents who had the same idea.

"They are heading up the peak!" screamed a white-faced British lady, and the cry bounced like a loose tennis ball from one tense knot of watchers on to the next.

"No, no," I called, trying to pull out the panic button. "They are only going to Government House. It is the governor they want, not us."

But, curiously, my reassurances did not bounce at all. It was as if these people enjoyed their fright and planned to savor it right there in our road all afternoon.

To each his own, I thought. Who wants to sit on a hillside with a flock of frightened females? They will scare themselves to death and enjoy it thoroughly, but that's not for me.

I ran back into the house and called to Ahyee, our Chinese baby-amah who had joined our family soon after our arrival.

"I am up here, Missy," came her gentle voice from upstairs.

She appeared at the top of the stairs as I went up. Her face, usually serene, was now blanched with fright but she kept her composure admirably.

"I am with Dana," she said quickly. "He is fine, don't worry. I closed the windows so he can't hear the noise. He is not frightened."

"Good." I smiled. "Thank you, Ahyee. But don't you worry either. Nobody is coming up here."

"But what is going to happen, Missy?" she asked, watching me closely, hoping for further reassurance. "Will the Communists take over Hong Kong?"

She had been through this before in Shanghai and she was naturally frightened. That had been in 1949, and as the Chinese Communists swept in to take over the city, she and her family had crept out and gone to Hong Kong as refugees. Her husband, Ahwoo, was now our cook, and their three daughters lived with us too: one attending school and the others holding jobs of their own elsewhere. Now, with the danger spreading to Hong Kong, Ahyee was grateful that they were all safely together, but Hong Kong was the end of the road. There was no place to run to from here.

"No, no," I said, putting an arm around her small shoulders, "that can't happen here. Mr. Hangen says that they just want to talk to the governor. He is sure that they won't bother us."

Ahyee relaxed a bit and said, "I will stay with Dana anyway, Missy. Don't you worry either." And she smiled and turned back to the nursery.

How lucky we are to have you with us, I thought, following her into Dana's room. He was on the floor balancing blocks as we entered his room. He looked up, said something unintelligible, and laughed happily. Ahyee squatted down beside him and put another of the wooden squares into place. The peace of the room seemed to defy all the terror in town.

I stayed there playing with them for several minutes, but then my curiosity got the better of me. I had to know what was happening down there where Welles was. Trees blocked the view from Dana's window, so I went out to the side of the house and up a ladder to the roof. There, from a quiet spot in the eaves, I spent most of the afternoon watching the rioting in town. My binoculars caught it all.

Well, not quite all. I did *not* see Welles caught in a mob of several hundred truculent rioters. Nor did I see him ducking angry blows as shattered glass sprayed through the air.

"How in the world did you get away?" I asked that evening.

"I didn't," he said. "I hung a big red Mao button on my lapel and we went right on filming. They thought we were Communists too, so we were left alone. The camera was jostled a lot but I think that we got some good shots. The mobs were pretty nasty until the police moved in with teargas. That moved them out fast."

Welles laughed then and said, "You would have loved the tourists, though. They thought it was some kind of Chinese folk festival and kept snapping pictures until they were frightened

174

away. One old gal started to complain about the smog until she heard that she'd just been gassed. She got out of there fast."

Hong Kong and its tourists had stumbled into a critical situation without fully understanding what was happening or why. But unlike Macao where the government simply gave up, the British remained calm, resolutely straddling the fault, and as it turned out the Communists alienated so many Hong Kong Chinese by their frenzy that they lost any mass support they had.

It was right about then that "Saturday Night at the Maos' " became a part of our lives.

China was still sealed to American newsmen, and most others as well. The only way that Welles and his colleagues could get reports out of that tormented country was by monitoring Chinese broadcasts and sifting through reams of newsprint from the mainland. If this was dull fare for writers, it was at least adequate. But for television newsmen, it was hopelessly pallid.

"There must be a way to get film from there," Welles said as he clicked off the local newscast one night. Then he stopped abruptly, whirled, and turned it on again.

"That's it!" he exclaimed. "Why didn't I think of that before!"

"We've been watching a Hong Kong news program, sweetie," I reminded him, finding it odd that he should be so confused. "It didn't originate in China, you know. They do that here."

"I know that," he said, shooting me the look I deserved. "But Canton has a television station and it is only seventy-five miles away. Why can't we pick that up here?"

"The mountains block it?" I offered.

"The mountains block it," he answered flatly. "They are right in the way. But let's go to the top of the mountain, the highest one, Taimoshan. I would wager a bet that we can pick it up from there."

"You can probably see Canton itself on a clear day, but what does that have to do with . . ." I began, but he had already left the room and was wildly dialing the hall telephone.

"Lim-san?" I heard Welles say, talking to NBC cameraman Lim Youn-choul. "Do you think that you could get broadcast-

175

quality pictures by filming programs from a television set? Good. Now, could you do it with some sort of power-pack on top of a mountain? Excellent! My friend, we have us a plan."

And they did. But it almost disrupted our home.

Lim and his NBC camera colleague, Yoshihiko Waku, are brilliant technicians and they proved it once again. They put together two 12-foot antennae, a kinescope camera, and two portable television sets, thereby constructing a machine for filming Chinese Communist telecasts originating in Canton.

To obtain a direct line of sight to Canton's transmitter, a clearing on the wind-swept summit of Taimoshan was chosen as filming site. It was a full hour's drive from the office, and because the Hong Kong government would not let them set up a permanent installation, they had to set up and dismantle the unwieldy gear for each filming session. It was a voracious time consumer.

Worse yet, Canton's programs came in lengthy transmissions three nights a week with no advance schedule available. And since they included segments from all over China, a missed show might mean losing something important. So from that time on, they watched every program. Summer, winter, rain or shine, our men were on their mountain.

Welles' description of those fog-bound nights remains with me still.

"I often felt that the rest of the world had vanished in the mist," he said. "Our small band of men, huddled around that flickering screen, swathed in heavy clothing against the cold, looked like a party of snow-blind hunters, mesmerized by the last feeble light in a world of darkness."

But they got splendid film of China, and for the first time viewers in the United States could watch actual events happen in that sealed land. So the scheme paid off, and we even found that dining at midnight three times a week has its romantic attractions.

"Saturday Night at the Maos' " was a coup for Welles and his crew, but it has been a source of regret to me ever since. I never accompanied Welles to his lonely mountain top even though I knew how important it was. Wind-swept peaks have never been especially appealing, and I thought, as the nights went by, that there would always be another time.

24

We Always Come Back at Night

China was not our only troubled neighbor at the turn of this decade. We were surrounded by agonized countries, all writhing in distress. It was like living in an intensive care ward during a plague. And the doctors were all out.

Vietnam's pernicious influence throughout Indochina was impossible to isolate. It infected Laos when North Vietnamese supplies flowed down the Ho Chi Minh trail within her borders, enroute to armies in the south. It spread to Thailand with the buildup of U.S. bombing missions operating from there. Russia and China locked horns over mainland passage of Soviet arms to North Vietnam. Even Korea caught the bug when our troops and planes were siphoned off to aid Saigon. It seemed that Cambodia alone was immune.

Prince Norodom Sihanouk of Cambodia was having his troubles too, but he had been playing one off against the other for so long that they seemed dwarfed. The prince was like a ringmaster, passionately fond of surprises.

"I will keep maneuvering as long as I have cards in my hand," he announced in late 1968. "First a little to the left, then a little to the right. And when I have no more cards to play, I'll stop."

The cards ran out for the prince fifteen months later with his precipitous ouster from power. With all his neighbors embroiled in war, Sihanouk's brand of neutrality was caught by the plague and finally succumbed.

We were old Asia hands by this time, having chalked up three more years in Hong Kong. Claire, our beautiful Cradle daughter, had come to join us the previous year and our family circle was complete.

On our trip back to the States to adopt Claire, Dana, who was then three, made it clear that he intended to have a hand in choosing his sister. He knew precisely what he wanted, having conducted a serious study of little girls for weeks. If he had been given his way, we would have adopted a dozen or more pretty girls, straight off the park swings in Hong Kong.

"I want yellow hair and spots," Dana announced as we returned from another study session on the playground one morning. I hoped that he meant freckles; measles we didn't need. "She has to push my swing and my pedal-car and wash my dog and . . ."

"But darling, she'll be just a baby," I said, laughing. "She won't be able to do much of anything for a long time. She probably won't even have much hair at first. But okay, we'll try to make it yellow."

Dana was thoughtful for a moment. Then he frowned and said, "Puppies are better. I want a puppy instead."

"Hey, sport," I said, hugging him, "we already have a dog. What we want is a little sister, and we shall have one. You will just have to wait a little while for her to grow. Then you two will have lots of fun together. You'll see." And I kissed him and the subject was closed for the moment.

On the next go-around, Dana decided that he wanted a big brother instead and he continued to be pretty firm about that until we got to the Cradle. There, seeing blond, six-week-old Claire lying asleep in her bassinet, he was mesmerized and could hardly wait to take her home. And during the first weeks after our return to Hong Kong, he spent hours by Claire's crib, blowing at the Jack-and-Jill mobile and squeaking her toys. Anything to get her attention and to make her smile. He even showed her picture books, and seemed to consider himself her guardian.

Then came the inevitable.

Welles and I were having breakfast one day, sitting on our

179

verandah overlooking the harbor. Suddenly Dana burst in, furious and on the verge of tears.

"Daddy! Mommy!" he said angrily, almost shouting, *"why* we chose Claire? She is a terrible terrible girl. Let's take her back. She is *so bad!"*

It was all we could do to keep from laughing out loud at this study in righteous indignation. Welles took Dana onto his lap, and after much hugging and tickling, our son seemed mollified. Smiling again and feeling much better about himself, he left to return to Claire.

"What do you suppose *that* was all about?" Welles asked. "He was angry enough to take Claire apart."

"Ahyee was probably giving her more attention than she was him," I suggested. "I think that our little boy has suddenly discovered that there are other fish in the sea. And he's not at all sure that he likes it."

"Whole books have been written about that," Welles said, nodding. "I guess we'll just have to give him a lot of extra attention for a while."

"Let's hope that takes care of it," I agreed. Then shook my head. "He's a great little guy, honey. Reminds me of you."

Welles looked at me for a moment and then laughed too.

"The temper?" he asked. "Yes, well, I'm doing better with mine, thanks to you." And he leaned over and kissed me, and went back to his breakfast.

That had been over a year ago. Welles' China-watching had kept him mostly in Hong Kong since then, so his suitcases were gray with dust. I thought that they looked lovely that way but . . . there does come a time.

"I'll do it, Daddy," Dana called, bouncing through the bedroom door with dustcloths in hand. I guessed that Ahyee had equipped him. "Let me dust them. Please?"

"Thanks, tiger." Welles smiled. "Make it one bag this time. I won't be gone long." And he watched fondly as Dana pounced on the two-suiter and pulled Claire up on top of it after him. She was now nineteen months old and determined to copy her brother in everything he did.

180

Then: "Easy does it!" Welles said. "If you smash the bag now, the airline won't have any fun. Come on now, *off.*" And he hauled it up on the bed to pack as the children left the room, already busy with another game.

"I can't imagine Cambodia at war," I mused, remembering those gentle people and their lovely country from a vacation we had enjoyed there not long before. "It's the most peaceful place I have ever seen."

"Not now," Welles said, shaking his head. "Sihanouk's neutrality was great while it lasted. But now all stops are out."

"All he ever wanted was Cambodia's independence," I reasoned. "Who could disagree with that?"

"Nobody, as long as it worked," Welles explained. "But his aides saw him leaning toward the Communists, and blew the whistle. I am afraid that the Cambodia we knew will never survive."

Welles was right. The witches of Endor themselves could not have foreseen more dire developments.

Prime Minister Lon Nol requested American intervention. On April 28, 1970, American and South Vietnamese troops swept across the border into Cambodia under cover of planes and artillery fire. The aim was to scourge a fourteen-mile border area of Vietnamese Communist sanctuaries inside Cambodia. But it brought a tragic consequence instead: they merely drove the enemy deeper into the country. By the end of the operation, whole areas of the north and south were under Communist control and solid Viet Cong pockets dotted the whole country. What had been a border headache was now a malignancy afflicting all of Cambodia.

Prince Sihanouk, exiled to Peking, had been forced to choose sides. He now considered himself head of Cambodia's Communists, the Khmer Rouge: a force which he had earlier viewed with antipathy. The balancing act had stalled left.

Welles was now in Phnom Penh. His letters told a grim tale. Empty markets and growling stomachs were turning the placid Cambodians surly. The government needed a scapegoat and found one helplessly handy: the resident Vietnamese. Racial

181

fervor drumming through the country led to wholesale massacres, and bullet-riddled bodies floated down the Mekong like aphis-ridden leaves on a stream. Everywhere people were plunged into a frenzy of chauvinistic hatred. Far from restraining the chaos, the Cambodian Army reflected it. They had little food, less direction, and no pay. Morale was stillborn. And communications among fighting units were almost nonexistent. Even army headquarters in Phnom Penh was late in charting troop movements, and their intelligence circuit of Communist action was a joke. Newsmen trying to link up with Cambodian troops to report the shifting front had to rely on hunches. There was little solid information even from advance American and South Vietnamese positions. But military spokesmen held daily briefings anyway and the newsmen all went, hoping that the vacuum would fill.

"They usually only confirm what we have already reported," Welles wrote. "It is not really clear who is briefing whom, but it's reassuring to hear that we were right.

"Nothing here is serious," he added, "only catastrophic. Why don't you come next weekend and see for yourself?"

How marvelous, I thought. There was nothing in the world I would rather do. The newspapers were full of stories about newsmen being killed or disappearing while reporting the Cambodian invasion. It sounded like a particularly hazardous story to cover, and although I knew that Welles was always careful, I wanted to see for myself. I couldn't wait to pack.

First in the bag were five tins of tuna to perk up my husband's rice-benumbed taste buds. Then, a supply of chalk and opium which is Asia's answer to cod liver oil; a few handipacks of water purification pills, and three of Dana's best dinosaur watercolors. All would be presents for Welles, whose physical *and* spiritual props surely needed shoring. Then I carefully folded his favorites among my dresses, and went off to have my hair done: bonuses for the spirit, to Welles with love.

The children painted pictures right up to departure time. There was enough artwork to paper the whole Phnom Penh hotel, but Dana pressed another into my hand as I was leaving.

"Daddy might need this," he said as he kissed me goodbye. It was a very drippy picture of a big brown tank, carefully camouflaged.

"Daddy will love them all," I assured them, "just as he loves you two. Dana, Claire, take care of each other. And don't forget to feed Igloo. Ahyee will watch over you while I am gone. It will only be three days."

With bright smiles they waved me out of sight.

It should have been a short trip but our plane stopped first at Siem Reap beside the Angkor temples in northern Cambodia. All passengers were tourists except me and this was their goal. It was a clear, bright day in May, and on our descent the panorama of looming gray shapes, some obscured by entangling vine and others grandly isolated, was enthralling. I was so immersed in the sight that I didn't notice the soldiers massing at the airport until our wheels touched down. Then they swarmed onto the plane. The captain announced that the soldiers were Cambodian government troops, sent to guard the plane. Welles hadn't mentioned trouble in Siem Reap! Whatever Phnom Penh had to offer would be better than this spooky place. Forty-five minutes later we took off. But this time I was all alone in the cabin, the only passenger flying on.

It was difficult to get from the plane to the Phnom Penh terminal when we finally arrived. The staff kept trying to give me transit cards, urging me back on the plane to return to Hong Kong. When I said that I planned to stay in Phnom Penh, they looked at me as if I had taken leave of my senses.

But then I saw Welles. He was smiling broadly and waving both arms wildly above the crowd. And once again, with great joy, I knew that this trip was right.

Together. Even the grimness of Phnom Penh at war was lightened by the simple fact of being together. So much to talk about, so much to share. Those three long weeks of separation were over!

Welles' colleagues were all around the arrival hall when we walked through, but I wasn't surprised that we were not introduced. That would come later. I was aware of their warm

183

smiles, and saw some clap Welles on the back as he hurried me through to his car. Then we were in each other's arms, unmindful of hooting taxis behind, nagging us away.

Later, in our hotel room, Welles hung his art gallery like splashes of brightness over drab beige walls. When the last was up, he gazed about proudly.

"The little troops are good, honey. They must take after their mother with all this talent."

"The only thing I can draw with confidence is a five-pointed star," I told him. "No dear, you are the brains and beauty in our family. I'm good at other things."

"It has been a long time," Welles said, drawing me into his arms again, "but I remember."

Welles left early the next morning with NBC cameramen Yoshishiko Waku and Roger Colne. Cambodian soldiers were trying to retake Ton Le Bet on the banks of the Mekong, and the newsmen wanted to film the battle. It would be an important one because the town faced Kompong Cham, the strategic former capital which had been threatened by Viet Cong troops. Flushing out Ton Le Bet would strengthen the larger city's defenses. Failure to do so would amount to a stunning victory for the enemy. Welles wanted to see the outcome for himself.

They did not plan to return until late afternoon, so I set off to explore Phnom Penh.

The city had changed terribly since our last holiday there. Then the streets had been spotlessly clean. Prince Sihanouk was obsessed with hygiene and sent garbage collectors out three times a day. Now those lovely broad avenues were cluttered. Mounds of trash listed in every alley and clans of lively rodents fought for possession. The silence was eerie. Formerly effervescing with crowds of cheerful people, Phnom Penh's streets were now vacant and still. The central market still bubbled with humanity but even there a hush came at mid-morning when a curfew sent everyone home. The stalls were different too. Once crowded with jewelry, hardware, or food, now they all sagged under piles of clothing, all of it olive drab. Young men clustered around, pulling pants and shirts, jackets and boots off the heaps,

184

holding items up for size. Cambodia's young were dressing for war, and they had to pay for it themselves.

Nearby tourist shops had given up on silver, and instead showed soldier hats and mounds of chevrons, battle ribbons, and insignia pins. Soldiers rummaged through the piles of decorations and became distinguished veterans on the spot. Walls of wet sandbags blocked government buildings and armed soldiers lounged at the door. Even post office customers were frisked and the telephone office was completely off-limits unless one carried a pass. I returned to the hotel wholly disheartened.

As I sat in our room reflecting on all I had seen, the door flew open and Welles strode in. Waku and Roger were with him and all three were radiant.

"We really hit it this time, honey," Welles sang out, swinging me around in his arms. "Cambodian troops took the town all right. Chased the Viet Cong clear out. And we got it all, exclusive. The competition was a full hour behind us."

We were prancing around the room by this time, but try as I might, I could not find their wavelength. Exciting? The whole thing sounded incredibly dangerous to me and I didn't like it at all.

Waku was on the floor, his arms stretched deep in a light-proof cloth bag, changing his camera film. Roger was labeling the film cans for shipment to New York. And Welles began to record his narration.

Cambodian troops, trained in South Vietnam by American Green Berets, have dislodged the Viet Cong from the Mekong River port of Ton Le Bet in an amphibious operation that took more than a week.

No American advisers were visible because the town lies beyond President Nixon's limit for U.S. penetration of Cambodia. But American planes were often heard overhead.

Ton Le Bet was reduced to rubble by Cambodian artillery and South Vietnamese bombers after the Viet Cong were reported in the city. The 15,000 residents had fled. Ton Le Bet now ranks as the most thoroughly destroyed Cambodian town.

By the time Cambodian troops finally entered Ton Le Bet, most of the Vietnamese Communists had slipped away. . . .

185

Another victory like Ton Le Bet may be more than Cambodia can stand. If the Cambodian people have anything to say about it, they may prefer to be overrun by their enemies than ravaged by their friends. When it comes to looting, pillage and general piracy, the Vietnamese Communists are about on a par with Cambodia's eager defenders from South Vietnam, even when the defenders are ethnic Cambodians. The sacking of Ton Le Bet will help convince many Cambodians that ideology has little to do with this war and that their real enemies are simply outsiders, especially outsiders from Vietnam, north and south.

This is Welles Hangen, NBC News, in the former city of Ton Le Bet, Cambodia.

It had been a long hard day, so by the time the newsmen shipped their film, fatigue took over. Welles and I canceled our dinner plans, bid our friends good night, and closed up shop quite early.

I had not planned to worry Welles with my fears, but just before we went to sleep, suddenly they all spilled out.

"This whole thing scares me," I said abruptly. "So many newsmen have disappeared on those lonely roads and others have been killed. Darling, you have put in more than your time here. Can't you please come on back home and let someone else take over?"

Welles looked at me closely.

"You don't ever have to worry, honey," he said quietly. "We are always very careful. We stop at every checkpoint and in every village to ask about danger ahead. If there is, we go back. We are looking for Cambodian troop movements, not trouble."

"But would they know?" I persisted. "About trouble ahead, I mean?"

"If the Viet Cong is around, everybody knows," Welles said. "The jungle grapevine sounds it loud and clear.

"And another thing," he continued. "Some reporters stay out in villages overnight, to be ahead on the story next day. We never do. Too risky. No," he said firmly, "we always come back at night.

"And I don't think that we will be here more than another week anyway," he added.

"Oh Welles, really? Just one more week and you will come back home? That is marvelous!"

I knew that sleep would come sweetly this night, for the first time in weeks. Neither of us could know that it would be the last sweet sleep for a long, long time.

The Chinese Embassy staff was expelled from Phnom Penh the next day. Welles and I were at the airport to watch the exodus and record it for television. My own plane back to Hong Kong would follow their departure, so we took my luggage along. In one hand I had Cambodian Army hats for the children, and a portrait by Roger Colne in the other. The picture resembled Ho Chi Minh, and a near-riot ensued when the airport crowds saw it. Rumor spread that I was leading a demonstration for the North Vietnamese, so I quickly stashed the portrait. A spy rap at that moment was something I didn't need.

Welles perched on a waiting-room bench to write his narration when the Chinese left. He pounded his typewriter briskly while I helped Roger package the film. Then I sat down to wait.

My flight was called. Welles still typed.

The flight was called a second time. Welles' typewriter blazed away.

"Will passenger Hangen on flight two-nine please clear customs!" the nasal voice implored.

I did not move. Welles wanted this film shipment to go along with me on the flight to Hong Kong in order to speed it to New York. There was no point in rushing him. He would finish when he was finished.

"Last final call for flight twenty-nine!" called the voice, warming up for the "final last call" which I knew would follow.

Then Welles jumped to his feet, ripped the paper from his machine, and raced for the departure gate. I ran along beside him, reaching for the script like a relay runner grabbing the baton. A quick kiss, an unwieldy film bag thrust into my arms, and I was through the gate. A passport stamp later, I headed across the tarmac to my plane.

Stumbling under the weight and bulk of my carry-ons, I looked back up to the observation deck. Welles was there, smiling happily, waving both arms in the air. A pack mule can't wave back, I thought, trying to get my breath. So I bowed instead, and the shift of my ballast almost flattened me. Everybody was laughing now, including me, as I trudged on to the plane. It was probably the merriest if least graceful departure Phnom Penh airport had ever witnessed.

Welles straightened his arms then, high over his head. With a kiss into the wind, he gave me a joyful victory salute.

He was magnificent that moment. I can see him still. Joyous, loving, vital. Aware of a job well done, he was completely at peace with himself and with the world.

A week later the phone call came.

"Welles went to Takeo yesterday and has not come back," the voice said. "It is about fifty miles from Phnom Penh. He probably decided to spend the night. I just wanted you to know."

Tears clouded my eyes.

"I am sure that you are right," I said slowly. "He *will* be back. Call me when you hear anything, please?" And the voice clicked off.

Then I became aware of the children, watching from the bannister. I brushed a hand across my eyes and managed a smile. "It's all right, darlings," I said huskily. "It's just that . . . Daddy probably won't be coming home as soon as we thought." I gathered them into my arms and cried, inside.

For the room had filled with a single sound: Welles' clear, vibrant voice.

"We always come back at night," he said, the words repeating, repeating, resounding off the walls.

We always come back at night.

When word came that Welles was missing in Cambodia, nobody had to tell me. I already knew.

For Welles had told me himself.

25

Then Came the Silence

Just the night before I had been watching Welles on television. It was his excellent Ton Le Bet piece being repeated. He looked so fine and happy. I was enormously proud of him.

Now, only a few hours later, he was reported missing. They said that he had driven off into the Cambodian jungle to cover a story. Exactly as he had been doing every day for weeks. But this time he stayed.

Now the jungle was silent. There was no trace of him at all.

I began wandering the house vacantly, talking out loud, asking the same questions over and over, praying somehow to be heard.

"Where are you, my darling? Are you all right? Please God, is he all right? Welles! Welles, where *are* you?"

Then suddenly I felt a warmth, a curious calming warmth that seemed almost physical. It was as if gentle hands had laid a soft shawl around my shoulders to protect me from the chill of fear.

And I *knew.*

Welles was alive! He might have been captured, and might be a prisoner, but he was alive. I knew it. I even seemed to hear his voice.

"It's all right, baby," Welles said to me, deep within my mind. "Try not to worry. I will be back."

I took a deep breath and looked up at the sky. A parade of fluffy white clouds was floating slowly westward. Westward toward Cambodia. Toward Welles.

189

"Give him my love," I murmured. "And tell him that I heard."

Tears were streaming down my face.

"We'll win this one too, my darling," I said and gave Welles our victory salute, with arms stretched up into the sky. And then collapsed to the floor, senseless with sobbing.

Grief can be borne only with activity, and fortunately the next morning I *had* to pull myself together, for there was much to be done. The news of Welles' disappearance had not yet been made public and our families in the States had to be informed quickly in advance. I would have phoned them but was afraid to trust my voice. So cables went out instead:

WANT YOU TO KNOW BEFORE THE NEWS BREAKS THAT WELLES APPARENTLY WAS CAPTURED SUNDAY IN CAMBODIA. TRY NOT TO WORRY TOO MUCH, AS I HAVE ALL FAITH IN HIS ABILITY TO GET OUT ALL RIGHT AS I KNOW YOU DO. I'LL KEEP YOU INFORMED OF ALL LATE DEVELOPMENTS. BLESS YOU AND HIM.

Then, wearing my bright red linen dress for courage, I headed for town where another job needed to be done.

Our friends at the NBC News bureau in Hong Kong were in a state of gloomy despair when I walked in on them. Maria Ling, the beautiful Macanese office manager, was in tears at her desk. Office messenger Cheong stopped his mail-sorting and stared at me, white faced, as if he were seeing a ghost. Reporter Bob Green abruptly ended a phone conversation and got up from his desk to meet me.

"Hey, you guys," I began, smiling as brightly as possible, "it's going to be all right. Welles can take care of himself in *any* situation. You know that as well as I do. And when he comes back he's going to have a great story. He will lead the Huntley-Brinkley Show every night, and you all know it."

Bob had his arm around me now and gave me a hug. Maria dried her eyes and tried to smile. Cheong was still a white frozen figure but a thaw had set in.

"Is there anything new, Bob?" I asked as we went together

into his office. "Do you know anything more?"

It turned out that Welles was not the only newsman unaccounted for in Cambodia that day. Both Yoshihiko Waku and Roger Colne were missing with him. And a CBS crew of television newsmen had also disappeared. Somehow this news seemed reassuring. At least Welles was not alone. One man conceivably can vanish without a trace, but not eight. No one knew where they were but I felt confident that they were safe.

Returning home that afternoon, I found a string of strange cars parked in the driveway. The children were off with Ahyee, swinging in a nearby playground, so I knew that they were all right. But something odd was going on in our house.

I ran up the stairs to the front door and found it standing open. An ashen-faced Ahwoo was just inside, all but hiding behind it. There, in the front hall, was a mob of reporters from Hong Kong newspapers. Some were scribbling in notebooks while others were snapping pictures around the house. There was even a television camera set up in the living room!

I wanted to *scream*. Go away and leave us alone! Don't you see that you are only making things worse?

But I didn't scream. The irony was clear: This was the other side of the news coin and today, for us, it had come up tails.

The business is not always kind, as I well knew. These reporters were on assignment and had no choice but to come. They had a job to do and it was obvious that they didn't like it any better than I.

So I said, "Good afternoon, gentlemen," and entered the hall, stepping past Ahwoo who was mumbling apologies. "I am Mrs. Hangen. May I help you?"

Clearly embarrassed, they too began to apologize for the disturbance and introduced themselves.

"I understand why you are here," I said then. "But your story is about my husband and his colleagues. Not about us." I smiled, looking at each in turn, and said, "We have two small children who don't know anything about this. They think that their father is simply off covering a story. They expect him back soon. And so do I."

One reporter started to ask a question, thought better of it, and said instead, "We're sorry to have bothered you, Mrs. Hangen. Truly. And we hope that Mr. Hangen comes back very soon."

With that, they all headed toward the door, murmuring apologies and good wishes.

Then I said, "Look, if it will help, I'll be glad to phone your editors and explain. Because I do appreciate your understanding our situation."

They all brightened considerably at this. "It sure would," one said. "Thanks a lot!" And they all left smiling.

When the door closed, I leaned against it and took a deep breath. My thoughts tumbled over each other: Dana and Claire must be protected at all costs . . . they are much too young to handle uncertainty. . . . They can't read newspapers . . . our friends won't tell them. Yes, it *can* be done.

I couldn't know how important this decision would be for *me* in the days to follow. For the children were to become my greatest strength.

David Brinkley broke the shocking news to NBC viewers that night on the Huntley-Brinkley Report. Walter Cronkite told the story on his CBS News program. Eight more newsmen lost while covering the American intervention into Cambodia was the lead story. Now millions of viewers shared our tragedy. And newspaper readers around the world would soon join in. Bad news moves like the Red Ball Express. I prayed for courage enough to handle the days ahead.

Telephone calls began flooding in early the next morning and continued all that long day. Cables too, and later letters by the scores. It seemed that everyone Welles and I had ever known was gathering around, as if to bridge our separation with their support. Messages filled with confidence, certain of Welles' return. Our friends knew, with me, that his remarkable wealth of inner resources could bring him through anything safely.

192

I had long felt that the people of NBC were our extended family. They proved that now. Everyone went to bat for Welles and his colleagues, thinking of ways to help. And they enfolded the children and me in warm protective wings.

Jack Reynolds was one. It was he who brought word that Welles was missing. Dread news was never more tenderly told.

Jack was in charge of the NBC Tokyo bureau then but had come to Hong Kong on special assignment. This was a blessing for me. There was never a more sympathetic man. Nor a wiser one, for he turned our disaster into a challenge when news came three days later that our men had indeed been captured and taken prisoner.

It happened May 31, 1970. In a hired white van with its Cambodian driver, Welles drove away from Phnom Penh in the early morning. As usual, Yoshihiko Waku and Roger Colne went with him. They didn't know that five minutes ahead of them on that road to Takeo sped a jeep and a blue sedan.

The jeep paused at a checkpoint, then continued on south. The sedan stopped too, but went on through. When the white van came into view, the guards waved it on. They assumed that the three cars were traveling together. But to Welles the signal meant something else: There was no need to stop, for it was all clear ahead.

They drove on, unmindful of danger.

Minutes later, rounding a bend in the road, they came upon the stalled blue sedan. Kojiro Sakai and Tomoharu Ishii of CBS stood in stunned silence beside it.

Then a thundering explosion. The white van stopped and our men leaped to the ground.

"The jeep has been hit!" someone shouted.

"What the hell do we do?" a voice screamed.

But the time for decision had passed.

Viet Cong troops sprang out of nowhere, cocking their rifles, surrounding the cars. An ugly "hands up" in Vietnamese, a few barrel prods, and then a forced march away.

The five newsmen trudged single file into the jungle with Viet Cong in command. They had been impeccably careful, but there is no armor against fate.

For Jerry Miller, George Syvertsen, and Ramnik Lekhi, there was none either. Those three CBS newsmen died in their jeep. With that explosion, the world lost three fine reporters. The five who were marched away, the world lost too. If only for a while.

None of this would be known had a miracle not happened: Welles' Cambodian driver escaped back to Phnom Penh. He brought the heart-lifting news that the five men had marched off to a jungle hut where they were given a warm meal. Then, accompanied by a uniformed officer, they were driven away with disciplined troops, not guerrillas. This was important. The Cambodian was left behind. That was the last he saw of them.

The story was taken up later by a farmer who had himself been held prisoner for a time. He said that Welles and his colleagues were brought to a house near Wat Po pagoda, which shows clearly on Cambodian maps. He talked with them most of the night. They seemed relaxed, certain that they would be identified as noncombatants and soon released.

Early the next morning our five men were taken to the pagoda for further questioning. The farmer never saw them again. At Wat Po we lost the trail.

Now we were facing a blank wall.

Viet Cong troops swarmed Wat Po. No one dared venture in. Until Cambodian troops could clear the area, there was no way to discover more. They were our only hope. We were wrapped in helpless frustration. Was there nothing to do now but wait?

Then, once again, Welles' strength and love coursed through me and came to our aid. In the shadows of my silent thoughts, I asked him what to do.

"If our positions were reversed . . . if I were the missing one . . . what, my love, would *you* do?"

And the path opened up.

We began Operation Cablegram. Anyone who might have connections beyond the battlefront was urgently cabled. We

194

cited Welles' credentials as a bona fide newsman and begged for help in getting him and his colleagues released. Some to Hanoi, others to Peking. Paris, Vientiane, New Delhi, Stockholm, Bucharest, Moscow. To presidents, prime ministers, and princes; to educators, journalists, generals. All beseeching help.

Bob Green and Maria Ling found new names. On the cables flowed. NBC New York and our bureaus around the world increased the traffic's hum, and soon it seemed there could be no one on the planet who had not had the word.

We could not know for certain who Welles' captors were, but we thought that they were Viet Cong troops. There were thousands in the area, although Hanoi disputed the charge. There were also dissident Cambodian forces, including the Communist Khmer Rouge ostensibly led by Peking-exiled Norodom Sihanouk. So we directed most of our appeals to Prince Sihanouk, and cited those when repeating our pleas to Chinese and North Vietnamese leaders.

I remembered our dark days in Egypt when Welles was barred from that country, and I could hear Bill Landrey's voice again as he counseled: "Everything must be done quietly, behind the scenes, without leveling blame. If you crowd anyone, you lose . . ."

The wisdom of those words was even more applicable now. We were trying to reach unknown captors behind enemy lines in a war zone. Trying to strike a responsive chord somewhere out there in a place we could not reach. And we had to go through third parties because we had no identifiable addressee.

We were in the complex position of working to preserve the options of the very people responsible for our troubles. It was frustrating as hell. But any accusation or blame would jeopardize the lives of our men. There was no other way. So on we went.

In most parts of the world, newsmen are assumed to be spies unless proven otherwise. This had to be tackled first.

Julian Goodman, chairman of the board of NBC, issued a statement which expressed the point precisely:

Welles Hangen, one of our most distinguished foreign correspondents, is missing in Cambodia. We are using every possible avenue to get word about him, thus far without success. But it is clear that what might most endanger him is the unfounded suspicion that he is in any respect an agent of government, rather than the independent professional journalist he has always been.

So every appeal that went out stressed Welles' integrity first and then asked for help. Most of the responses were positive. Many brought new ideas and offers of further contacts. But none had any information for us.

Jack Reynolds and I culled Welles' scripts for the best proofs of his objective reporting. Each script specified camera work by Waku and Colne. Bob Green made French translations, and we sent those out by the scores. We felt that all bases were covered and prayed for quick results.

But, again, none came.

Instead we began to get rumors.

"They have found two graves near the ambush site," Jack Reynolds began somberly when he came to the house one morning. "They think that one of the bodies is Welles. But Pat, would Welles have been wearing a blue checked shirt? And did he usually wear black shoes?"

"He always went out in a bush shirt," I said quickly. "Khaki. And his shoes are brown. I am certain."

Then I jumped up and raced upstairs. With a heavy chill, I remembered that Welles had one blue shirt with checks and a couple of pairs of black shoes. If they were gone from the closet? That would mean that they had been packed.

I was afraid to look, but I had to. Tugging open the shirt drawer, I saw only white. I dug deeper. It was there! The blue checked shirt was there in place. And the shoes? There they were, shiny and black! My heart soared at the sight.

"It's all right, Jack!" I called down the stairs. Then, taking them two at a time, I said, "Welles' things are here! He has only these, and they are all here!"

But Jack looked solemn as I entered the room. Our eyes met. We both knew what had to be done.

"Can you get Welles' dental charts?" Jack asked quietly. "It is the only way to be sure." I nodded, finding no words. And we left the house together.

The bodies had been taken to a pathology lab in Saigon, so we sent the charts there along with those of Waku and Colne. It would take until tomorrow to get the results. The night was endless.

Jack and I bent breathlessly over the NBC telex next morning as it started to hum. Click, click, clack. Saigon was warming up. The seconds dragged like minutes. Then the impersonal clicking letters began to form words, marching deliberately, one after the other.

"Proved . . . proved positively . . . no repeat no identification Hangen Waku Colne . . . bodies Cambodian villagers . . . death: natural causes."

We hugged each other and cheered. Then suddenly I began to cry. Tears of immense relief. But tears also of prescience: We had disproved this report, but it would not be the last. A precedent was set, not a finality established. There would be many more erroneous stories before we could find the truth.

I remembered Mark Twain's comment in a similar situation: "Reports of my death are greatly exaggerated." And he went on to live a long, long life.

I took a deep breath, dried my eyes, and smiled. At least we now knew the Mark Twain route. And something more: We knew that it could be handled.

26

When Phnom Penh Falls...

It was then that the messages began to come.

Hong Kong was like the Lisbon of World War II, the seat of intelligence operations for everybody. On the surface it was a tourist's dream: exotic, glittering, filled with enchantment. But beneath the veneer lay a network of intrigue labyrinthian enough to make Ian Fleming switch to cookbooks.

China was still closed to the outside world; most of Southeast Asia was at war, and Russia was extremely interested in the affairs of the whole continent. So there were resident agents, double agents, and agents' agents behind every other pair of chopsticks. It was *the* place to be if you needed information.

There was a certain Mr. Brown living in Hong Kong who was overtly engaged in custom clothing, but he was so well plugged into the underground that he all but owned the switchboard.

I knew that Welles had great respect for Mr. Brown. He was an honest man who had lived in the Orient most of his life and had an innate ability to penetrate the inscrutable. He was modest and thoughtful, and I knew that Welles had often checked out rumors with Mr. Brown and had never been disappointed in his assessments. So I hurried to enlist his help.

Welles' high regard for Mr. Brown proved mutual. He was eager to make inquiries through the Communist underground, a convoluted network that led to informed sources in both Peking and Hanoi.

"It may take a while to get anything," Mr. Brown said, "if in fact we do. They may not reply at all, but it's worth a try."

198

I agreed and promised to be patient. If any news came, Mr. Brown would simply leave a message for me that he had called. Then I was to meet him at eight o'clock the following morning in a popular coffee house in the heart of town and he would relay the news.

"It is always best to meet in a crowded place," Mr. Brown said with a slight smile. "It gives a casual tone to the encounter and assures privacy."

So it was arranged and we parted. Then I headed for Kaitak airport to get Welles' bag.

NBC had kept Welles' Phnom Penh hotel room in readiness for several weeks after he disappeared. Then, feeling that his things would be safer at home, they air-freighted his suitcase back to me. But it did not arrive.

The airline sent tracers out on it but days went by without a report. Now they thought that they had it. A suitcase answering the description—gray Samsonite with a strip of red tape pasted along the top for quick identification—had been found in Bangkok and they shipped it on to Hong Kong. It was waiting for me now in the airport office. I was anxious to claim it and take it safely home.

The Kaitak freight office was a warren of wooden crates and ceiling-high cardboard packing boxes. I edged my way through to the counter and found a clerk.

"You have a dark gray suitcase that just arrived from Bangkok," I began, pulling from my purse a copy of the air freight order. "I have come to pick it up."

My hands were beginning to shake so I quickly put the paper on the counter. The thought of seeing Welles' things again was creating an emotional turmoil that was hard to control. I tried to calm myself as he took the paper into the room beyond. Moments later he returned with Welles' suitcase.

I reached for it but he stopped me, saying, "There is no identity tag so we will have to open it here to be sure that it is yours. May I have your keys, please?"

"I don't have them," I said, "but I am sure that is my husband's bag. I put the red tape on it myself."

But the clerk shook his head. "Against the rules," he replied. "But we could break the locks, if your husband wouldn't mind."

I nodded. "Do, please," I said. "I am sure that it is ours."

The clerk put a little pick under one lock and pried it up. Then he forced the other, and the bag opened.

It was full of bright pink jumbo-sized hair curlers with pink satin ribbons! Dozens of them, crowding the case. Just hair curlers. Nothing more.

One look was enough. I turned quickly away. I knew then that Welles' suitcase was lost forever. With his things, his personal things which I wanted so badly to treasure.

The clerk was watching closely, waiting for my answer. But sobs choked my throat. Shaking my head wordlessly, I hurried for the door.

"Gosh, lady," the clerk said, "I'm sorry. I didn't know that it was so important."

The drive back home from Kaitak took over an hour and I needed the time. Just to be alone. I had a lot of work to do— on myself.

"It doesn't matter," I said aloud. "It really doesn't matter. We can replace Welles' things when he comes home."

But it *did* matter. Welles was missing. And now so was his suitcase. It mattered terribly. You build up your emotional defenses so carefully and then they are shattered by some new shock. Like those pink hair curlers. And you are right back at scratch again.

But I was learning that every time emotional defenses are rebuilt, they are strengthened. And by the time I reached home, I felt like a reconstructed armadillo. The layers of surface protection, at least, were intact.

Fortunately a busy afternoon awaited me. A Harvard professor was in town on his way to Hanoi. This was another reason for my staying in Hong Kong: People traveling to China or North Vietnam invariably came through. It would help if they could be persuaded to ask their Communist hosts about Welles. We needed any information we could possibly get, and most travelers willingly complied.

Today's visitor, however, was unusually taxing. He had only two hours before continuing on to Hanoi, and there was just one thing on his mind: He needed a camera. He could speak of nothing else. Not even missing newsmen. Not until he found the right camera.

Jack Reynolds offered to help in the selection, and I tagged along hoping for an opportunity to discuss Welles' disappearance. The minutes flew by. The professor could not decide. Then, just as I was losing hope, the choice was made, cash changed hands, and the professor was delighted. He was so proud of his camera, he was prepared to do anything we might ask.

When he left for Hanoi, the Harvard professor was carrying a thick folder of documents, pictures, and scripts. The Vietnamese would hear, once again, that the world outside wanted Welles Hangen back.

Jack took me home then. As we parted, he asked gently, "Think you can keep it up?"

I ran a hand through my hair. "Of course, Jack," I said. "What else do I do? Maybe *this* time the word will get through."

It was about a month later that I returned home from town one day and found the message that Mr. Brown had phoned. This was it! We had a message from the Communist underground at last!

Early the next morning I dressed carefully and hurried toward my rendezvous with Mr. Brown. At exactly eight o'clock I walked through the coffee house door. The place was jammed with customers and was humming with talk. I peered through people and smoke, searching for Mr. Brown. Then I saw him, sitting alone at a small table in the back, all but obscured behind a newspaper.

I made my way through the crowd, jostling and being jostled, stepping aside for hurrying waitresses, and finally reached the table. Mr. Brown smiled and stood up to greet me. He helped me to be seated, ordered coffee for us both, and then leaned forward across the table.

"I have a message for you," Mr. Brown began quietly. "It

201

came from a high Communist Party official in Peking. It is cryptic but very interesting."

He was searching the inside breast pocket of his jacket as he spoke. Then, finding the paper he wanted, Mr. Brown pulled out a small memo-sized page, glanced at it, looked at me, and smiled.

"I am to tell you that the captive journalists will be released very soon, provided that they don't become a political issue. The source mentions Welles by name and says that he will be one of the first to be released."

I closed my eyes for a moment.

"Thank God," I said softly. "He is still alive. And they know where he is, or they wouldn't have said that. They didn't have to answer at all, did they? But they did. And mentioning Welles by name . . . oh Mr. Brown, it is *wonderful!*"

"In the Chinese Communist lexicon 'very soon' could mean a month or more," Mr. Brown cautioned. "And with the emotional movement in the States about the POWs, this warning about political involvement is significant. You must keep a clear distinction between the missing journalists and the military prisoners, you know."

"We have been doing that all along," I said quickly. "The newsmen were not a part of the war at all. They were reporting it from the sidelines. None was politically involved. As you know, they weren't even armed."

"Can you keep the distinction?" Mr. Brown asked. "And make sure that everything that is written about the newsmen makes that point?"

"Yes, definitely," I answered. "Do you think that they may release our men as a good will gesture? Because they are disturbed by the POW uproar at home?"

Mr. Brown reflected a moment.

"I think that could well be it," he said finally. "Let me put a few questions back through the circuit and see if we get something more. I'll be calling you again, you may be sure."

I really floated home after that. We were finally getting somewhere!

I suppose that it was this surge of optimism that made me

202

decide to accept an invitation that night. The children and I usually spent our evenings together, but this night an old friend was in town and had asked me out for dinner. I thought it might be a good change. Perhaps I had been keeping too much to myself. And anyway, I had big news that should be celebrated.

Dana and Claire perched on my bed, watching me dress.

"You look beautiful, Mommy," Dana said as I fastened the zipper of my blue dinner dress. "Why don't you wear that all the time?"

"Because I don't go out to dinner all the time," I said, laughing. "This will be an early one, though, with an old friend of Daddy's. A nice man whom we haven't seen in years. He has to leave for India in the morning so I guess you won't meet him. But maybe next time."

"Are you going to a restaurant?" Dana asked, having just discovered the enchantment of eating out.

"Will you bring us something?" Claire wanted to know.

"Probably," I said to Dana. "I will if I can," I promised Claire. Then I gathered them into my arms and kissed them. "Ahyee will tuck you in when it's time. And don't worry, I won't be late." And I went off for my date in town.

Our friend was staying at the Mandarin, a hotel in the busy central district of Hong Kong island. I called his room from the lobby housephones, and he suggested a drink up there before going on to dinner.

I felt almost happy as I rode up in the elevator and walked down the hall to his room. I could hardly wait to see him and to discuss Mr. Brown's message. And when he opened the door at my knock, we hugged each other warmly.

"Pat!" he exclaimed, drawing me inside. "Gosh I'm glad to see you. You look absolutely great!" And he took my coat and ushered me into the room. Bar supplies were set up on the dresser, and a Chopin waltz came softly from a corner cassette.

"Look at that view, sweetie," he said. "Isn't it fantastic?"

I crossed the room to admire the harbor while he mixed martinis for us. Then he joined me, handed me my glass, and raised his in a toast.

"Here's to us, to being together again," he said, slipping his arm around my waist. It wasn't exactly the toast I would have chosen under the circumstances, but I let it pass. "A great view," he went on, "and a lovely lady to share it with. I've really been looking forward to this."

"Do you know?" I said, smiling at him, "I haven't felt so happy in months." And I was just about to tell him why, when I felt his hand slide down from my waist to the base of my spine.

I turned, taking a step away, and faced him.

"There is good news I want to tell you," I said. I wasn't about to let a wandering hand spoil this evening. "A man named Brown here in Hong Kong has a message from—"

"Why are you wearing a panty girdle?" he broke in. "You don't need one, not with that figure. Come"—he took my hand— "let's sit down. We can see the view more comfortably from here." And he led me to the bed.

Am I imagining this? Our good old friend actually making a pass? No, I guess I've been alone too much.

Surprised at myself and feeling a bit foolish, I took a sip of my drink and sat down.

"Sweet sweet girl," he said softly, taking my glass, putting it aside, sitting down on the bed next to me. "How lonely you have been, and how very brave. Let me help you. I don't want you to be so alone." He put his arms around me and started to pull me back on the bed.

"No, stop!" I said, pushing him away. He was a big man but not very agile, so I had little trouble getting up. "This is ridiculous. Come on, pull yourself together and let's go have some dinner."

"Hey, Pat," he said, laughing, trying to pull me back down to him. "Where's the harm? My wife won't mind. We're all good friends. And a little loving will do you good. Come on, baby. I just want to help."

"Damn you!" I said, suddenly furious. "You just don't know, do you? You have no idea what it's all about. You sure have changed, old friend. Welles wouldn't even know you now." And I was out the door.

Hurrying back down the hallway to the elevators, I felt

deeply insulted. This sort of thing happens to other women, but not to *me*. Everyone knows how I feel about Welles. Or maybe I'm just kidding myself, thinking that they understand. Or maybe, just maybe *this* man was never our friend at all.

Then I was in my car heading for home. Tears rolled slowly down my cheeks and I didn't try to stop them.

Damn you, I thought wearily, as I drove the winding road up the peak. Damn you anyway. You sure know how to hurt a person. Well, maybe it is better *my* way after all. Just staying home, waiting for it all to end. It will someday. God willing, one day it *will end.*

I went straight up to bed when I got home, but sleep would not come. I lay rolling, tossing, aching. Desperately lonely for Welles. Sobbing and aching. Finally sobbing myself to sleep.

But sometime in the pitch black of night, I awoke again. At least partially. I thought that there was a knock at the door, then a pounding, insistent, increasingly insistent, growing louder and louder.

I got up and went downstairs to the front door. Taking off the latch, half-asleep I opened the door. There, standing in the doorway, was Welles . . . gray, empty-eyed . . . holding up both hands pleading . . . haggardly pleading for help. Then he faded away. And I fell to the floor, losing all consciousness in a swirl of darkness.

I don't know how long I lay there. When I came out of my faint, I was limp and icy cold. The door stood wide open. Moonlight shone on empty steps. A strong wind swept through the hallway. Stiffly I got to my feet and quietly closed the door. Then, leaning on the bannister, I climbed slowly up to bed.

But the dream, and its horrible apparition, went with me. And would return and return, to live with me from that night on.

The months continued to crawl by, and with no further word from Mr. Brown. I devoted myself to intercepting travelers and to contacting others who might be able to help. Influential people were now being invited to Peking, and I cabled them all, asking their help.

205

Edgar Snow was one. Few Western writers were so welcome in China as he, and he wrote me from Peking:

> I read with great sympathy your telegram expressing concern about Welles Hangen and other journalists missing in Cambodia. Prince Sihanouk has just told me that he is genuinely distressed that he cannot help legitimate journalists. He said that he received your appeals and has done all he can but has no information. One can only hope that in this case no news is good news—as has so often proved true of missing persons.

The wall of silence seemed impenetrable, but I felt that with such expressions of concern we would at least keep up the pressure. And if people of influence continued to ask, one day answers *must* come.

Ping Pong diplomacy opened China to American newsmen in 1972. Jack Reynolds and NBC correspondent John Rich were two of the first to go to Peking. At last we had direct communication with the Chinese, and with Prince Sihanouk. Both Jack and John prodded for information and were assured that further investigations would be launched.

Then came President Nixon's visit to China. The many American correspondents who accompanied him intensified the search.

Walter Cronkite was a member of that press party, reporting the historic journey for CBS. He was also chairman of a committee of newsmen who had joined together to help find their missing colleagues, and he carried along a bundle of documents and pictures which he distributed widely.

Barbara Walters accompanied the President too. Before she left for China, she wrote me: "There is some possibility that I may be meeting with Prince Sihanouk. If so, I'll certainly ask him or anyone else I meet about Welles. He is in all our thoughts. I pray that this fantastic trip brings us good news for you."

Dana was in the hospital having his tonsils out when that historic China trip ended. I was reading him stories, hoping to take his mind off his aching throat, when a nurse signaled me to come to her telephone. Walter Cronkite was calling from New York.

"How is Dana?" Mr. Cronkite asked first, with concern.

"He is getting along just fine, thank you," I said, "but how are *you?*"

"A little tired," Mr. Cronkite said, "because we just got off the plane from China. I didn't want to wait before calling you because I know you're anxious to know what happened. But I'm sorry to say that there is not much to report."

My heart sank at that, but Mr. Cronkite went on.

"We brought up the subject with everyone we met," he said. "It was all pretty high level and they did agree to investigate. But of course they said again that it is a Cambodian problem, not theirs."

"Did they accept the brochures and pictures of the missing newsmen?" I asked.

"Yes, they did," Mr. Cronkite replied. "That much is good, but I wish that I had something more encouraging to tell you."

"The fact that you *asked* is the important thing," I said quickly. "When people like you show concern, they can't ignore it. This could be a real breakthrough."

"Well, I hope so, Pat," Mr. Cronkite concluded. "I'll keep in touch. Take care of yourself and those great kids."

I sat quietly there at the nursing station for several minutes after that, trying to sort my thoughts. I had hoped for so much more. For almost two years we had been forced to work through third parties because none of us could get into China or Hanoi. Now a group of American newsmen, friends whose own prestige was enhanced by the power of the presidency, had talked to high Chinese officials directly, but had learned nothing. I had not expected them to bring Welles *back*, but I had hoped that they might find out where he was. And how he was. And get somebody to tell *somebody* to release him.

Then Mr. Cronkite's warm voice came back in my mind, and I thought how really fortunate we were that such people cared. He had picked up the phone himself the minute he returned, in spite of all the things he had on his mind.

207

"I am sorry, Mrs. Hangen," a nurse said, breaking into my thoughts. "Dana is crying. I think that he needs you."

I had forgotten where I was.

"Of course," I said, getting up quickly. "Thank you, nurse. I'll go back to him now." And I hurried down the hallway to our son's bedside.

The poor little boy was sobbing and coughing miserably.

"It's all right, sweetie," I said gently, taking his hand. "I know it hurts a lot now. But that means you're getting better. And soon you will be well again and back playing baseball with your gang. Look," I continued, choosing a book from his stack, "here is your favorite story about Babe Ruth. I'll get you some ice cream and then let's read it together, shall we?"

And we did, the whole long afternoon.

When I returned home that night, I found that Mr. Brown had called again. Another message through the Communist underground! Could the questions asked in Peking by our press friends be having an effect already?

It turned out that this new message was even more cryptic than the last.

"The newsmen will be released," it read, "when Phnom Penh falls."

Good God, I thought. Phnom Penh? This is ridiculous. Phnom Penh is in just about as much danger of falling as Toledo, Ohio!

I couldn't know that Cambodian insurgents would surround that capital city, pull back, and then surround it again. And again over and over, for the next many months. And that finally it would indeed fall.

It was a message that I tried very hard to forget as I watched the Lon Nol government reel from blow to blow. I put it out of my mind every time our government propped him up, in anticipation of the next crisis. He had to give in eventually, but when? And might it not then be too late?

As the number of crises mounted, each fading for a time only to become more ominous, the message continued to haunt me. Even though Phnom Penh eventually fell, the message haunts me still.

27

Who Among the Missing

"When is Daddy coming home?" Dana asked one morning as he, Claire, and I were building a block dollhouse on the floor of their room.

"As soon as he can, darling," I answered, as I always did.

The question had been asked countless times. The children still did not know the truth.

"How long has it been since he went away?" our son continued.

"Over a year now, honey," I replied. I had never lied to either child. If a question was asked, I always tried to answer it honestly but simply. Then I would wait, with some apprehension, for the subject to be pursued. It never was.

But I knew that one day it would be, and then I would have to tell them both the full story.

Dana frowned now, thought for a moment, and then said, "Mommy, maybe Daddy got married again and doesn't want to come back."

That did it. Clearly this was the day.

"No, darling," I said quickly, placing another block in position. "Daddy is married to us. He loves us and wants very much to come home. And he will, when he can."

Thank God we are working with our hands, I thought, so that this can be as normal as possible.

"Daddy went to Cambodia to make television pictures of the war, as you know," I began slowly. "In wars, people sometimes get captured by mistake. We think that is what happened to

Daddy. He was with Mr. Waku taking pictures of soldiers fighting, and some soldiers from the other side took them prisoner."

Dana was balancing a block on the dollhouse roof now, and Claire was searching for one of a certain shape to complete a column. Neither child said a word but they were listening intently.

"But darlings, we know that the soldiers are taking good care of Daddy," I said, choosing my words carefully. "They took him to a house and gave him a good dinner. And Daddy is not alone. Mr. Waku is with him, and some other friends too. So even though he misses us, it is good to know that he's not lonely."

"But why are they keeping him there?" Dana wanted to know. The big question that none of us could answer.

"We just don't know, honey," I replied. "We think that they may want to trade Daddy for something very important that they want from the Cambodian government. But we can't be sure."

It was awfully weak, I knew, but there wasn't anything else to say.

Dana thought that over for a moment. Then he said, "I go to a British Army school. Maybe I could ask the British soldiers to go find Daddy."

"That is a fine idea, dear," I said. "But the British are doing a lot to help Daddy already. The Queen of England herself wants Daddy back."

That was bending the truth a little but I didn't think the queen would mind. Donald Hopson, the British chargé d'affaires in Peking, had been one of our best liaison men with the Chinese for months. And British government officials here in Hong Kong had been enormously helpful all along.

"So are the French," I continued. "The president of France went to China and asked about Daddy. He is trying to find him too."

Just the month before, Pierre Mendès-France had begun new inquiries personally in Peking. The former French president had already sent us several messages and was hopeful that his

210

intercession might bring news. The French ambassador to China, Etienne Manac'h, had also been consistently helpful.

Then Dana asked, "Well, what about President Nixon?"

I had to smile at that. There had indeed been a recent exchange but it was not especially gratifying to remember. President Nixon had mentioned the missing newsmen in the course of a major foreign policy speech, and hoping that he might have had some response, I sent him a cable:

MR. PRESIDENT:
MY HUSBAND WELLES HANGEN OF THE NATIONAL BROADCASTING COMPANY IS ONE OF THE EIGHTEEN INTERNATIONAL JOURNALISTS MISSING IN CAMBODIA WHOM YOU SO COMPASSIONATELY INCLUDED IN YOUR SPEECH TODAY. I BELIEVE THAT YOUR CONCERN FOR THESE JOURNALISTS CAN BE EXTREMELY EFFECTIVE IN GAINING INFORMATION ON THEIR WHEREABOUTS AND WELFARE AND IN OBTAINING THE ULTIMATE RELEASE OF THESE MEN. MAY I EXPRESS MY GRATITUDE ON BEHALF OF OUR CHILDREN AND MYSELF FOR YOUR CONCERN. SINCE IT HAS BEEN IMPOSSIBLE FOR US TO OBTAIN ANY CONFIRMED INFORMATION ABOUT MY HUSBAND, I WOULD BE DEEPLY GRATEFUL IF YOU COULD INFORM US OF ANY NEWS THAT MIGHT COME FROM YOUR VERY MOVING APPEAL.

A week later, the response came. It was written on White House stationery and signed by the President himself. I opened the envelope with great excitement and read:

Dear Mrs. Hangen:
Your comments about my new initiative for peace in southeast Asia were especially gratifying to me. I greatly appreciated your very thoughtful message and I hope that our efforts to reach an honorable and enduring end to the war will merit your confidence and support.

But there was no point in dwelling on that now. Dana was waiting for an answer to his question.

"Honey, I'm sure that President Nixon is doing everything he can to help us find Daddy," I hedged. "Why, he even sent us a Christmas card, remember?"

The children were quiet then. It seemed that the questions had stopped.

211

"Many many wonderful people all over the world are trying to help Daddy and to bring him home," I said. "One day it will happen. I am sure. Any other questions?"

The children shook their heads.

"Well, whenever you do have any, just ask and I will tell you everything I know. Okay?"

They nodded. Then Dana said, "Oh, just one more question, Mommy."

"Sure, dear," I said. "What is it?"

"When we finish the dollhouse, may we go to the playground?" he asked.

"Oh yes, please?" chimed in little Claire.

So our session was over. As children will, Dana and Claire had accepted it all with innate pragmatism. There would be many more questions in days to come, but I knew now that there would be nothing that could not be answered. I was immensely proud of them both.

As those months in Hong Kong became years, the children and I recorded mountains of cassette tapes and took miles of movie film which we carefully stashed away to await Welles' return. I didn't want him to miss a single stage of the children's development, and both Dana and Claire seemed to find a special closeness with their father whenever the recorder or camera was turned on.

We never dated these chronicles, I think because I was finding dates increasingly difficult to face as time went on. Instead we recorded annual events in Hong Kong to set the time frame. Chinese New Year was a distillation of firecrackers popping and the sound of lion dancers in the streets. Our traditional Autumn Festival was marked by the laughter of children whose voices suddenly hushed as their lantern candles were lit. And for New Year's Eve, we recorded the deeply moving harbor symphony which rises from the whole expanse of Hong Kong harbor on the stroke of midnight. Hundreds of ships blowing, tooting, and honking in their uniquely orchestrated salute to the new year.

The NBC News bureau sent camera crews to Dana's and Claire's birthday parties. They produced delightful documentaries suitable for prime time on anybody's network, but they were ours alone to keep for Welles. I suspect that those parties were listed as "Saturday Night at the Maos' " kinescopes in the office accounts, but I never asked. They would help Welles to catch up on these missed years as nothing else could.

Whenever NBC thought it useful, I traveled to New York and Washington for consultations. With the help of the network, several eminent people made time available to talk about our missing men.

I remember U Thant most warmly. Pauline Frederick, the gracious lady who covered the United Nations so brilliantly for NBC, made the appointment, and she and I went together to meet this gentle Burmese who was then the secretary general.

As we entered his tranquil office on the top floor of the United Nations building in New York, U Thant rose from his desk and welcomed us. Leading the way to a comfortable corner overlooking the city, he invited us to join him for a quiet talk.

"I am distressed by the news of your husband," the secretary general said softly. "Have you heard anything at all?"

"No, nothing yet," I replied, conscious of deep concern in those kind brown eyes. "But I believe that we will soon."

"Do you have reason to expect something?" he asked, looking at me intently. "Have you had some word?"

I told him about our messages through the Communist underground, but confessed that it was essentially a matter of faith since there had been no real information.

U Thant bowed his head slightly and closed his eyes for a moment. Then he looked up with the same direct gaze, and spoke of specific plans he had made to help. He obviously had given much thought to the missing newsmen and had made inquiry through many channels already. Then, as Pauline and I rose to leave, he stopped me with a hand.

"Mrs. Hangen," he said softly, "you are a Buddhist. I shall hope with you for good news soon."

As Pauline and I walked toward the elevator, she said, "You

213

know, with all of the problems U Thant has on his mind, he has taken this one as a real 'heart' cause. You may be sure that he will not forget."

That was the last time I ever saw that brave, gentle man, but I shall always remember him with deep affection.

Then it was January 23, 1973.

Back again in our Hong Kong home, the children and I were gathered on the floor in front of our television set. Something momentous was about to happen. It was important that we view it together and tape it for Welles. We were using his own Uher recorder, and Dana switched it on as I took the microphone, ready to set the stage.

"It is now the evening of January twenty-third," I began haltingly. "President Nixon is going to make a special address about Indochina."

My voice faltered. I had prayed so very long for this day and for what I hoped it would mean for us. But facing it was hard. Harder than I had anticipated. This *had* to be it. But if not . . . could that be handled too?

Dana and Claire were watching me, wondering at my hesitation. There was nothing to do but go on.

"We all think that this is going to be the cease-fire announcement," I went on, speaking into the microphone, speaking to Welles. "I will record it all so that we can listen to it together, my darling . . . when you come home."

President Nixon came on the screen. There was a moment of silence. Then he began to speak.

"Good evening," the President said. "I have asked for this time tonight for the purpose of announcing that we today have concluded an agreement to end the war and bring peace with honor in Vietnam and in Southeast Asia."

Southeast Asia! Did this mean Cambodia too?

"A cease-fire, internationally supervised, will begin at seven P.M. this Saturday, January twenty-seventh, Washington time," Mr. Nixon went on.

That would be Sunday our time, I figured, since Hong Kong is almost a full day ahead.

214

"Within sixty days all Americans held prisoner of war throughout Indochina will be released. There will be the fullest possible accounting of all those missing in action."

Throughout Indochina? This was fantastic! Absolutely marvelous! I held my breath as the President went on.

"It is a peace that not only ends the war in Southeast Asia but contributes to the prospects of peace in the whole world."

Could I believe what I was hearing? I wanted to, desperately, but how could all fighting stop in Southeast Asia if Cambodia and Laos were not consulted? Or maybe they had been. President Nixon *must* know what he's talking about.

But Welles' tape recorder disagreed. It stopped working right in the middle of the speech, just as Welles would have done on a hoax, and it stayed motionless until the end.

I hurriedly put in new batteries, trying to salvage the rest of this historic speech. But it was too late.

"I had it right in front of the television, honey," I told Welles when the recorder started up again, "but it didn't pick up the sound.

"What Nixon said is that there will be a cease-fire Sunday," I went on, "and a return of all prisoners throughout Indochina in the next sixty days. He didn't specify Cambodia, but the implication was there. So . . . we will just have to wait for the written agreement to really know.

"But it is *good* news, darling. At least . . . the war is going to be over."

Dana jumped up and sang out, "Daddy's coming home! Daddy's coming home! Mommy, why are you crying? *Daddy is coming home!*"

Claire joined in and they pranced around the room, as I sat sobbing on the floor.

How strange, the times we cry. I should be as happy and as relieved as they. But I felt so weary, so completely drained. I put my head down on Welles' tape recorder and let the tears simply flow. This was the end of something. Something else would now begin. But who knew what?

I wanted to believe Nixon, but I could not. This war couldn't end with his words. Some fighting might stop, but not all. Some men might come home. But not all. Then what? Then what do we do?

Suddenly the room was quiet. The children's voices had hushed. And I felt two small bodies pressing close, four arms wrapping round me. I looked up into solemn little faces and wide wondering eyes, and with a surge of gratitude I folded our beloved children close.

"God bless you," I murmured. This was no time to stop. Certainly it was no time for tears. This called for holding even closer, to each other and to our faith. For the next two months, at the very least, we would have to be stronger than ever.

"Darlings," I said softly, "you must both listen now. And listen carefully. We *hope* that Daddy will be able to come home, but we still don't know. We are going to have to be patient . . . a while longer."

For I knew that the next sixty days would seem an eternity.

Days of waiting, days of prayer. The endless days before we could know, at last, who among the missing would be coming safely home.

216

Epilogue

Welles was not on the list of prisoners that Hanoi eventually made public. None of the missing newsmen was named. And none came home with the returning prisoners of war. They remain silently missing.

So our search continues.

Somehow and someday, the Cambodian jungles will have to give up their secret.

Eighteen men do not simply vanish. Someone knows where they are. Someone has an answer. So we persist.

As with Welles' life, it is a search for truth. Unending.